WHY DO SO MANY INCOMPETENT MEN BECOME LEADERS?

WHY DO SO MANY INCOMPETENT MEN BECOME LEADERS?

(and how to fix it)

TOMAS CHAMORRO-PREMUZIC

HARVARD BUSINESS REVIEW PRESS

Boston, Massachusetts

378 3935

Copyright 2019 Tomas Chamorro-Premuzic
All rights reserved
Printed in the United States of America

10 9 8 7 6 5 4 3 2 1

The web addresses referenced in this book were live and correct at the time of the book's publication but may be subject to change.

Library of Congress cataloging-in-publication data is forthcoming

ISBN: 978-1-63369-632-7
eISBN: 978-1-63369-633-4

The paper used in this publication meets the requirements of the American National Standard for Permanence of Paper for Publications and Documents in Libraries and Archives Z39.48-1992.

To Mara Hvistendahl,
for writing Unnatural Selection,
the book that inspired this book

Contents

WHY DO SO MANY INCOMPETENT MEN BECOME LEADERS?

CHAPTER **1**

Why Most Leaders
Are Inept

Google "my boss is," and you'll see the following auto-complete options: "abusive," "crazy," "mean," "incompetent," and "lazy." Opinion surveys produce similar results. According to Gallup, a global polling firm that periodically collects attitudinal data from employees all over the world, 75 percent of people quit their jobs because of their direct line manager. Results like these reveal bad leadership as the number one cause of voluntary turnover worldwide. Meanwhile, 65 percent of Americans say they would rather change their boss than get a pay raise.[1] This shortsighted response fails to recognize that the next boss might not be any better, but worse.

What to make of the obvious fact that most leaders, inept or otherwise, are male? Since women make up around 50 percent of the adult population and, throughout much of the industrialized world, outnumber and outperform men in college, we might expect at least equal representation of women and men in leadership positions. And yet reality disagrees. In most parts of the world, the notion of leadership is so masculine that most people would struggle to name one famous female business leader. For example, in a recent survey, a thousand Americans were asked to name a famous female business leader in tech. Some 92 percent of respondents had no answer, and a quarter of the remaining 8 percent named "Siri" or "Alexa."[2] When I mentioned to a client that I was writing a book on women and leadership, her cynical response was, "You mean you are writing two books?" Her response typifies the weak association between women and leadership, and not just in people's minds.

Even among the S&P 500 companies (which are much more committed to gender equality than are smaller, privately held businesses), we are very far from seeing a balanced gender ratio. By 2017, the proportion of women in positions in these firms decreased as the power of the position increased:

44 percent of the workforce

36 percent of first-line and midlevel managers

25 percent of senior leaders and executives

20 percent of board members

6 percent of CEOs[3]

This book explores a central question: What if these two observations—that most leaders are bad and that most leaders are male—are causally linked? In other words, would the prevalence of bad leadership decrease if fewer men, and more women, were in charge?

I first asked this question in 2013, in a brief *Harvard Business Review* essay whose title summarized the issue: "Why Do So Many Incompetent Men Become Leaders?"[4] I argued that the underrepresentation of women in leadership was not due to their lack of ability or motivation, but to our inability to detect incompetence in men. When men are considered for leadership positions, the same traits that predict their downfall are commonly mistaken—even celebrated—as a sign of leadership potential or talent. Consequently, men's character flaws help them emerge as leaders because they are disguised as attractive leadership qualities. As this book will show, traits like overconfidence and self-absorption should be seen as red flags. But instead, they prompt us to say, "Ah, there's a charismatic fellow! He's probably leadership material." The result in both business and politics is a surplus of incompetent men in charge, and this surplus reduces opportunities for competent people—women *and* men—while keeping the standards of leadership depressingly low.

The audience for the article continues to expand year by year—it has quietly become one of HBR.org's most-read articles every year since it was published—and I received more feedback on it than on any of the nine books or three hundred other articles I've written in my career. Sadly, the popularity of the article reflects the vast number of people in the world who continue to witness incompetent leadership and to suffer from it. If you have ever worked in an office, then you have probably experienced a particular form of bad management displayed by bosses who seem unaware of their limitations and are clearly and unjustifiably pleased with themselves. They are overconfident, abrasive, and very much in awe of themselves, particularly in light of their actual talents. They are their own biggest fans by some distance.

Yet these flaws seldom hamper their career prospects. *Au contraire*. And because these bosses are more likely to be men than women, much of the popular advice for female potential leaders prescribes stereotypically masculine behaviors such as "believe in yourself"; "don't worry about what others think of you"; and, my favorite, "just be yourself," as if an alternative were even possible. (As a humorous version of the be-yourself advice notes, 'Be yourself; everybody else is already taken.')

A clear sign of socioeconomic progress is the business world's attempts to place more women at the top of companies. And few large Western organizations lack diversity programs, most of which include an explicit focus on gender.[5] The programs, however, primarily aim to help women emulate men, with the underlying assumptions that women deserve the same or can also do it. But how useful and logical is this goal when most leaders are in fact quite harmful to their organizations? Instead of treating leadership like some kind of glamorous career destination or personal reward for reaching the top, we should remember that leadership is a resource for the organization—it is good only when employees benefit from it, by boosting their motivation and performance. Elevating the standards of leadership—not simply having more women in charge—should be the top priority.

For the majority of employees around the world, the experience of leadership is undeniably far from positive. Their everyday work reality breeds anxiety rather than inspiration, burnout rather than empowerment, and more distrust than trust. And while the public may admire and celebrate the people who rise to the top, things are usually different for the employees who have to work for them.

The data bears out this pervasive discontent. In a 2011 study of more than fourteen thousand human resource professionals and other managers, the respondents rated barely 26 percent of their current leaders positively and only 18 percent of future leaders as promising.[6] Similarly, senior executives have little faith in the potential of those they regard as successors. A recent global poll exploring how boards evaluate their talent management programs—the very systems designed to identify, develop, and retain leaders—indicated that fewer than 20 percent of boards are confident that their organizations have a grip on their leadership problems.[7] And while this book will focus on organizational rather than political leaders, the situation is hardly better for governments and heads of state. Some 60 percent of people in the world believe that their country is on the wrong track, courtesy of their leaders.[8]

Women's paths to leadership are undoubtedly dotted with many barriers, including a very thick glass ceiling. But the more I have studied leaders and leadership, the more I believe that the much bigger problem is the lack of career obstacles for incompetent men.

As we will see, people tend to equate leadership with the very behaviors—overconfidence, for example—that often signal bad leadership. What's more, these behaviors are more common in the average man than in the average woman. The result is a pathological system that rewards men for their incompetence while punishing women for their competence. We need to replace our flawed leader-evaluation criteria with more relevant, effective criteria: some that predict actual performance rather than individual career success. Things will get better, not just for women but also for everyone else, when we start picking better leaders.

The consequences of bad leadership

An area of Buenos Aires nicknamed Villa Freud boasts the highest concentration of psychoanalysts per capita in the world. Even the bars and cafés have Freudian names, such as the Oedipus Complex and the Unconscious. Many of the residents are therapists, in therapy, or both. In fact, psychoanalysts are only allowed to be therapists if they are in therapy themselves. The requirement creates a self-perpetuating and ever-expanding universe of psychoanalysts and patients. It's like an inverted—and unhealthy—pyramid scheme. Every new shrink is another shrink's new patient, and the arrangement keeps both supply and demand perennially high.

I grew up in Villa Freud. Even our dog saw a shrink, though it was always clear to me—perhaps even to our dog—that the dog shrink was really dealing with *our* problems, rather than our dog's. When I had to decide on a career, the choice was almost inevitable: I had to become a psychologist.

Growing up in Argentina also nurtured my interest in leadership, especially the problematic type. A century ago, Argentina was the future. It was not just the land of opportunity, but also one of the richest countries in the world, with a GDP per capita higher than that of France and Germany. Yet Argentina has been in constant decline ever since, being one of the few perpetually devolving countries in the world. The main reason? One bad leader after another. So, I asked myself the obvious questions: How can smart and educated people make self-destructive leadership choices, political term after term, without learning the lessons from previous failures? How can rational people who have their own best interests at heart fall for charismatic con artists who promise them the impossible while pursuing harmful agendas and corrupt selfish interests? Although this depressing state of affairs eventually propelled me to leave Argentina, I promised myself that I would do what it took to understand—and help fix—this toxic side of leadership.

And indeed, today I am a leadership psychologist. Much of my work focuses on helping organizations avoid incompetent leaders and make the already-installed leaders less ineffective. The work has important repercussions. When you get it right, you see enormous benefits to the organization and its people. And when you get it wrong, you get . . . Argentina.

In business, a bad leader significantly affects subordinates by reducing their engagement—their enthusiasm for their jobs and the meaning and purpose people find at work. Global surveys report that a staggering 70 percent of employees are not engaged at work and that only 4 percent of these employees have anything nice to say about their bosses.[9] Quite clearly, good leadership is not the norm, but the exception.

The economic cost of disengagement is even more astounding. In the United States alone, lower engagement translates into an annual productivity loss of around $500 billion.[10] This estimate is probably conservative, since it is based on large multinational corporations: organizations that actually bother asking employees how they feel about their jobs and that devote considerable time and money to improve how their employees experience work. The average employee in the world is probably even more miserable.

Productivity loss is not the only downside of disengagement. Disengaged employees are also more likely to quit their jobs. Employee turnover incurs a huge burden, including separation costs, damaged morale, and productivity losses associated with the time and resources needed to find and train newcomers. Between 10 and 30 percent of the employees' annual salary is lost to turnover costs. The figure is even higher for replacing leaders, since top executive-search firms will charge around 30 percent of the leader's annual salary on top. And turnover is not always the worst-case scenario for businesses. When disengaged employees do decide to stay, they are more likely to misbehave, for example, abusing staff, bending the rules, and committing fraud.

Women as one solution to bad leadership

As this book will describe, reliable evidence shows that among leaders, women generally outperform men (see chapter 5). Most notably, in a review of forty-five studies on leadership and gender, Alice Eagly, a professor at Northwestern University, and her colleagues found that women were more able to drive positive change in their teams and organizations than men were, not least because of women's more effective leadership strategies.[11] Specifically, women elicit more respect and pride from their followers, communicate their vision more effectively, better empower and mentor their subordinates, approach problem solving in a more flexible and creative way, and are fairer and more objective in their evaluation of direct reports. In contrast, male leaders are less likely to connect with their subordinates and to reward them for their actual performance. Men focus less on developing others and more on advancing their own career agenda.[12]

Despite the typically small gender differences, the study concluded that "all of the aspects of leadership style on which women exceeded men relate positively to leaders' effectiveness, whereas all of the aspects on which men exceeded women have negative or null relations to effectiveness." The small but significant differences in female leadership all point in one direction. Where women are different, they perform better. Where men are different, they perform worse.

Of course, these findings may reflect what researchers call *sampling bias*. Because women need to be more qualified than men to gain leadership opportunities, studies reporting that female leaders are more competent than men may simply reflect that women face tougher challenges than men do to become leaders. Such studies—which we'll explore in this book—are usually held up as proof that standards are unfairly high for female leaders. But I would reverse the argument: standards for male leaders are not high *enough*. Since we all want better leaders, we should not lower our standards when we select women, but we should raise them when we select men.

For example, studies have shown that women are less likely to get job interviews than are equally qualified men. Simple experiments have clearly borne out this effect. For example, when a researcher at Skidmore sent out identical résumés for applicants named either Jennifer or John, John was perceived as significantly more competent than

Jennifer—and was offered roughly $4,000 more in annual salary—despite identical résumés in all other respects.[13]

Because of this bias, women take longer than men to reach the same leadership levels. For example, an analysis of *Fortune* 1000 CEOs showed that the tiny minority—just 6 percent—of CEOs who were women took 30 percent longer than their male counterparts to reach the top, which explains why female CEOs in these companies are on average four years older than their male counterparts.[14]

Paradoxically, then, we should not be asking, "If women make such great leaders, why aren't there more of them?" Because the logical answer to the question is that women are such great leaders because for women, it's much harder to become a leader at all.

As I will show, it's not just gender bias that holds competent women back from leadership and allows incompetent men to float to the top. It's a fundamental disconnect between actual leadership talent and our assumptions about it. There is a world of difference between the personality traits and behaviors it takes to be *chosen* as a leader and the traits and skills you need to *be able* to lead effectively.

Leading effectively versus being chosen as a leader

Justine—a real person with a fake name—is a smart and inquisitive Belgian accountant who has spent the last fifteen years working as the senior financial officer for a large nongovernmental organization. Although she has continuously delivered beyond expectations and is seen by her manager as one of the most valuable people on the team, she rarely promotes herself. Instead of networking and managing up, she prefers to focus on her job and perform each task as proficiently as possible, letting her accomplishments speak for themselves. When new projects come up, she volunteers for them—but only if she is absolutely sure she can deliver.

Perhaps it won't surprise you to learn that Justine has seen many of her colleagues get promoted ahead of her—even when they are not as good as her. But through their confidence and assertiveness, they convey the impression that they are not just more competent, but also more driven and leader-like. And since they can continue to rely on Justine to keep the trains running for them, their incompetence is often masked by Justine's silent but effective contribution.

Most of us know someone like Justine. Perhaps you even feel a bit like a Justine yourself. In fact, Justine's story is not an exception but the norm for many of us—both men and women. In any organization, individuals who focus on getting ahead of their colleagues are more likely to be rewarded by their managers than are people less driven, even if the ambitious individuals contribute little to the organization.

Someone I'll call Stuart—a former coaching client of mine whose name I changed—exemplifies this truth. He has enjoyed a stellar career in public relations and was recently hired by a big Silicon Valley firm to lead its external communications. Anyone who looks up Stuart online will be impressed by his résumé, network, and public brand: two TED talks, past senior roles in three *Fortune* 100 companies, and thousands of social media followers. However, none of these accomplishments reflect Stuart's ability to lead. In fact, most of his former employees would agree that as a leader, Stuart was primarily absent and had dismal management skills. But because Stuart devotes most of his time to manage his own reputation with the external world, he is a sought-after leader. And to further lubricate his undeserved career success, Stuart performs superbly in job interviews, coming across as driven and charismatic. Since interviews are the most common method for vetting leaders' potential, the future is bright for Stuart. Unfortunately, the same can't be said about the people who will have to report to him.

Recent research shows that people like Stuart—self-centered, entitled, and narcissistic—tend to emerge as leaders and take control of resources and power in a group and that these traits, which we'll explore further in chapters 2 and 3, are more common in men than in women.[15]

Freud provided a compelling explanation for the first part of this phenomenon, namely, that bad guys often finish first. He argued that a leader emerges when a group of people—the followers—have replaced their own narcissism with that of the leader, so that their love for the leader is a subliminal form of self-love. This projection of self-love will be especially common when leaders themselves are narcissists. "Another person's narcissism," Freud said, "has a great attraction for those who have renounced part of their own . . . as if we envied them for maintaining a blissful state of mind."[16] Look around, and you will find no better explanation for the rise of egomaniacs in politics, business, and elsewhere. We have created unspoken stereotypes of leaders as people—usually men—who seem oblivious to their weaknesses. And we have great tolerance for people—again, usually men—who are not as talented as they think.

Paradoxically, then, the same psychological characteristics that enable men to emerge as leaders may actually be responsible for their downfall. What it takes to *get the job* is not just different from, but also sometimes the reverse of, what it takes to *do the job*.

How odd, then, that so much of the recent debate over getting more women into leadership positions has focused on encouraging them to mimic the maladaptive behaviors of ambitious men. Do we really want to ask women to replicate a broken model?

How this book is organized

This book aims to help you identify the key qualities that cause people to become incompetent leaders—and, conversely, good leaders. By understanding the difference between the traits commonly associated with leaders and those that actually help leaders be effective, we can, hopefully, abandon the very selection criteria that are driving the epidemic of bad leadership. We can only stop what we can spot.

The next chapter examines one of the biggest causes for the bad-leadership epidemic: our inability to distinguish between confidence and competence, particularly when we try to infer leadership potential in others.

In chapter 3, we look at why narcissists manage to emerge as leaders and the consequences of narcissism on both the quality of leadership and the gender imbalance in leadership.

Chapter 4 examines the charisma myth. We tend to overrate the importance of charisma, a subjective inference based largely on someone's attractiveness or likability, as a key ingredient of leadership potential.

Chapter 5 discusses the female advantage in leadership. Because women have greater emotional intelligence than men do, women display more self-control, empathy, and transformational leadership when they are in charge.

In chapter 6, we look at the universal qualities that make leaders—both men and women—more effective. Although there are many models of good leadership, most of them highlight a few essential ingredients of leadership potential, such as expertise, intelligence, and curiosity.

Chapter 7 summarizes ways to evaluate the central elements of leadership potential. It focuses on data-driven tools that enable organizations to select better leaders by overcoming their problematic reliance on intuition.

Chapter 8 evaluates the effectiveness of coaching and development interventions designed to improve leaders' performance. While most organizations devote significant time and money to such interventions, their average success levels are disappointing.

In chapter 9, I present some final thoughts on the issues discussed throughout this book. I draw from lessons from the past and discuss the potential implications for gender-diversity programs in the future.

I hope you enjoy the book or that it at least debunks some of your preconceptions about gender and leadership. Please approach this book with an open mind and a healthy degree of skepticism. What you will read may bear little resemblance to others' ideas about women and leadership. Popular ideas include recipes for increasing gender diversity, such as asking women to step up, lean in, be more confident, or fake it till they make it. This book makes rather different suggestions.

Progress on the issue of female leadership has been slow and piecemeal. The time has come to consider a different solution, and that solution calls for a different type of analysis.

CHAPTER 2

Confidence Disguised as Competence

Shilpa and Ryan are team colleagues in a big global accounting firm. Although Shilpa is more qualified and experienced than Ryan, they are paid the same. Shilpa has been with the firm for five more years than Ryan has, but Ryan made such an impression during his job interview that he was hired at Shilpa's level despite being less qualified. His appointment is hardly surprising, given Ryan's interpersonal bravado. His self-regard is apparent not only during job interviews, but also in internal team assignments, client presentations, and networking events.

Ryan speaks more, and louder, than Shilpa does, and he is much more likely to interrupt other people in his enthusiasm to share his ideas, which he loves to present. He's less likely to qualify his statements with caveats and more likely to speak in bold strokes—something his boss sees as "having vision." When he and Shilpa present recommendations to clients, Ryan does most of the talking. When clients ask questions, Shilpa is likely to provide a range of options for further research and discussion. If she's stumped, she'll admit it. But Ryan never hedges. He usually comes up with a single recommended course of action. And if a client asks him something he doesn't know, he'll skillfully dodge the question.

Accordingly, their boss assumes Shilpa is less confident, and consequently less competent. Eventually, Ryan is promoted to a leadership role, while Shilpa remains where she is.

Sound familiar? That's because pretty much anywhere in the world—at least wherever data was gathered—we associate displays of confidence with leadership potential. Consider these examples:

> *Inc.com* tells us that "self-confidence is the fundamental basis from which leadership grows" and that "without confidence, there is no leadership."[1]

> According to *Forbes*, "confidence is always a leader's best friend."[2]

> The news website *Quartz* suggests that if only introverts could build some confidence, they might become leaders.[3]

> Virgin Group cofounder and business magnate Richard Branson assures us that the "secret

ingredient" that allows him to "rule and improve the world" is confidence.[4]

Entrepreneur challenges us to find "an extremely successful person who doesn't greatly believe in themselves. It's not going to happen. Steve Jobs, Martin Luther King, Jr., Michael Jordan, Elon Musk and Mark Cuban are just a few highly successful individuals who benefited greatly from this confidence."[5] (These people may have benefited, but what about the much bigger number of confident individuals who never become as successful, or even successful at all?)

I was recently invited to speak to a large global audience of executives who had been selected into a "high-potential" program for female leaders. The topic was gender and leadership. I began my talk asking the audience members to take a quick poll identifying what they considered the most important ingredient of leadership talent *according to science*. So, the question did not focus on their personal or subjective opinion, but reflected their knowledge of evidence and hard facts. The options included expertise, intelligence, hard work, connections, luck, and confidence. An astonishing 80 percent of the audience chose confidence, which is less important than all the others.

In this chapter, we'll explore two issues. First, we'll examine the relationship between confidence and competence. While most people look at a confident person and assume that the person is also competent, there is in fact no relationship between confidence and competence. Second, we'll burst some common myths about gender differences and confidence and what these myths really imply.

The difference between competence and confidence

How good do you think you are? Exceptional achievers are sometimes quick to attribute their accomplishments to their confidence. For instance, when Roger Federer, arguably the greatest male tennis player of all time, won his eighth Wimbledon title, he was asked by a BBC reporter to reveal the secret of his success. Federer's response? That it's all down to his confidence and self-belief. He believed in himself, and then he won. Really? Could it not be that his outstanding and exhaustively honed tennis skills played at least some role?

To be sure, there is no shortage of people with Federer-esque confidence, but they tend to lack the talent to back it up. Federer's achievements are unusual because of his talents, not because of his confidence. If I had to choose, I would rather have Federer's talents than his confidence, not least because talents lead to confidence more than vice versa. I would also rather have a boss, a taxi driver, and especially a heart surgeon who is competent rather than confident.

Competence is how good you are at something. Confidence is how good you *think* you are at something. Competence is an ability; confidence is the *belief* in that ability. Such belief or self-evaluations can refer to learned skills (e.g., singing, kissing, climbing Mount Everest, and managing people) or to personality traits (e.g., smartness, likability, persistence, and creativity). Our self-esteem is strongly influenced by how good we think we are. And the more important the task, the more it influences our self-concept. For instance, you aren't likely to get a huge ego boost from feeling confident in your ability to recognize a Justin Bieber song (perhaps the opposite?). Nor are you likely to berate yourself too much if you don't feel confident in your ability to speak Old Icelandic. If something doesn't matter to you, or is not highly valued by society, then it probably doesn't influence your ego. But if you are a mountaineer, whether or not you believe you can climb Everest will probably affect your self-concept.

In a logical world, the relationship between confidence and competence would be represented by a single circle in a Venn diagram, indicating that our self-concept accurately reflects our true competence. Alas, in the real world, confidence is rarely a sign of competence; the relationship is represented by only a marginal overlap between two distinct circles in a Venn diagram.

There is no simple of way of determining whether someone's confidence corresponds with his or her abilities unless you can measure the person's abilities. When people simply tell you that they are good at something, all you can do is guess whether they have accurately assessed their abilities and are telling you the truth.

Fortunately, hundreds of scientific studies have addressed this problem by assessing both how good people *think* they are (their confidence) and how good they actually are (their competence). For example, in a recent meta-analysis, German professors Alexander Freund and Nadine Kasten aggregated 154 correlations between people's self-rated intelligence and their actual intelligence test scores, including more than twenty thousand people in their analyses.[6] The results revealed that there is less than a 10 percent overlap between how smart people think they are and how smart they actually are. The finding has been replicated with a wide range of other abilities and competence domains (e.g., academic performance, musical talent, and social skills).

The prevalence of overconfidence

It may not surprise you that most of us overrate our skills and talents. Decades of research suggest that on virtually any dimension of ability, we tend to assume that we are better than we actually are.[7]

For instance, are you a better than the average driver? If you're like most people, you'll answer yes. Because even though it's a statistical impossibility for most people to be better than average, most people overrate their driving skills.

And it's not just driving. People see themselves as better than average across virtually any domain of competence—for example, cooking, sense of humor, and leadership—even though by definition most people are average. People also overrate their job performance, which explains why they tend to have trouble receiving negative feedback, even if they are lucky enough to have a boss who gives them honest and constructive criticism.[8]

Daniel Kahneman, the Nobel prize–winning psychologist who pioneered behavioral economics, summed up a great deal of his research by stating that "we are generally overconfident in our opinions, impressions, and judgments." What else is left? Not much. To illustrate this point, Kahneman and colleagues designed several brain teasers highlighting the problematic overreliance on intuition in our thinking. Here's one of the most famous riddles they tested:

A bat and ball cost $1.10.
The bat costs one dollar more than the ball.
How much does the ball cost?

This is a simple problem, but most people get it wrong because they trust their initial instincts more than they should. Even 50 percent of Harvard, Princeton, and Massachusetts Institute of Technology students come up with the wrong answer, which is ten cents.[9] The correct answer is, of course, five cents, and you don't have to be an Ivy League student to work that out. However, we are so confident in our intuition that we don't even bother checking whether our answer is right. And if we don't check our logic with brain teasers and other intellectual problems designed to trick us, think of how unlikely we are to do it with spontaneous social problems, where the answer seems much more related to our gut feeling than to any logical principle.

Although self-awareness—*knowing* how good you are—tends to increase with talent, one of the most astonishing findings in psychology is how little experts and clueless people differ in their self-perceived abilities.[10] The most inept individuals will also make the least accurate evaluations of their talents, grossly overestimating where they stack up against their peers. Meanwhile, the most competent people will exhibit much self-criticism and self-doubt, especially relative to their expertise.

For instance, in one study, students performing in the bottom 25th percentile of the class on tests of grammar, logical reasoning, and humor rated themselves as above the 60th percentile.[11] In contrast, top performers consistently underestimated just how much better they were than their peers. In the same study, people performing above the 87th percentile rated themselves as being in the 70th to 75th percentile.

The implications of these findings are clear: the more you know, the more aware you are of what you know and what you don't. Expertise increases self-knowledge, which includes awareness of one's limitations. Conversely, the less you know, the less aware you are of your limitations and the more overconfident you will be. As Bertrand Russell, the famous British mathematical philosopher and Nobel laureate, famously lamented in an essay condemning the rise of Nazi Germany, "the fundamental cause of the trouble is that in the modern world the stupid are cocksure while the intelligent are full of doubt."[12]

Why is overconfidence so pervasive? As with any other trait that is commonly manifested in a population, there has to be a benefit—an adaptive edge—to it, even if this benefit coexists with a counterproductive side. So, what is the benefit of overconfidence? It boosts or maintains our high levels of self-esteem. Our desire to feel good about ourselves surpasses our desire both to be good at something and to accurately evaluate reality, including our own abilities. For instance, although overconfidence has been linked to lower job performance, overconfident people tend to have higher self-esteem.[13] And while feeling better about ourselves does not change the reality of our talents, we humans have an inherent need to view ourselves positively.[14] A large meta-analysis of hundreds of studies and thousands of participants found that in almost 90 percent of scientific studies, people showed a consistent tendency to interpret events in a self-serving way. Need some examples? See if you can relate to these:

> You applied for a promotion but got rejected.
> What are you more likely to do? (a) Accept that
> you are not as good as you thought, or (b) blame it
> on the unfairness of your employer.

You go on a date and meet someone you like, but the person never calls you back. How would you typically react? (a) Accept that the person was just not that into you, or (b) conclude that he or she was not that attractive or interesting after all.

You get to your car to drive back home from a short shopping trip and find a parking ticket. What do you do? (a) Calmly accept responsibility and learn what you did wrong, or (b) blame it on the system that deceives drivers to make money out of them.

You are chosen for a leadership position even though you didn't expect to be considered. What do you assume? (a) That you were somehow lucky that your manager overestimated your potential, or (b) that you are really talented and deserve it.

You are fired from your job with little notice. What do you do? (a) Calmly ask for feedback so you can learn and avoid a repeat, or (b) try to understand why such an unfair decision was made, and continue until you have someone to blame.

You receive your annual bonus, and it's less than you expected. What do you do? (a) Accept that your contribution was not as significant as you thought, or (b) get annoyed that you are not appreciated.

As you may have guessed, most people would do option (b) rather than (a) across these situations, even if they don't admit it, and chances are you are like most people. Why? Overconfidence is the best way to cope with rejection and maintain a positive self-view when our status is challenged. For most of us, ego enhancement is a much better alternative than a brutal reality check.

Another reason for the pervasiveness and persistence of overconfidence is that it is an effective mechanism for deceiving others.[15] It is much easier to persuade others that you are better than you actually are when you have already managed to persuade yourself.

In this way, overconfidence can have self-fulfilling effects. The very fact of your being a leader can convince your followers that you are more competent than you actually are. This effect can create a virtuous cycle where people work harder to ensure your success. One study found, for example, that moderately overconfident CEOs were more likely to attract suppliers and investors and that their firms had lower employee turnover.[16] Overconfidence projected an aura of success and invincibility that bred real success simply because it led people to believe in it. Perceptions often create reality more than the other way around.

Does that mean that overconfidence is a good thing and that, as the self-help industry preaches, we should all visualize success and fake it till we make it? Not really.

Even if confidence helps us persuade others that we are competent when we are not, there are big downsides to having a distorted view of ourselves and our abilities. From knowing when to cross a busy intersection, to volunteering for difficult work assignments, to appearing on *America's Got Talent*, people will do better when they are not deceived about their abilities. As psychologists C. Randall Colvin and Jack Block note, "There is indeed a reality out there, and accurate perception of the relation between oneself and this reality is necessary for physical and social adaptation."[17]

Imagine that you are getting a root canal, and the dentist is coming toward your mouth with the drill. Would you rather that he or she was lacking confidence or competence? What about the pilot flying your plane or the financial adviser making investment decisions for you? When competent individuals lack confidence, they will prepare more, act with caution, and become more aware of potential risks and obstacles, all of which enhance their performance. When confident people lack competence, their best bet is to hide it from others. As you can probably see, even when confidence may bring career benefits to the individual—after all, you can fool some people all of the time and all the people some of the time—the advantages of confidence are less obvious for those who have to rely on that individual's performance. And remember, with just a 10 percent overlap between confidence and competence, you will often be forced to choose between the two.

Consider the most-cited form of overconfidence— driving. Overconfidence is one reason people drive when they are less sober than they think. It is also why they think they have time to drive through a crossing barrier before the train arrives or why they text and drive. In 2018, the American Automobile Association surveyed a thousand adults and found that 79 percent of men and 68 percent of women considered themselves better-than-average drivers.[18] In 2017, an estimated forty thousand–plus people in the United States died in car crashes.[19] Clearly, all of us would be safer if we had a more accurate view of our abilities, but we don't.

Women, men, and the two sides of confidence

As we've seen, even when our assessment of other people's competence is wrong, their self-confidence can still have self-fulfilling effects, opening doors and opportunities to those who simply seem more confident. This is one of the reasons that so many well-intentioned people have advised women to be more confident to get ahead at work and in their careers. There are several problems with this kind of advice.

First, it fails to recognize that confidence has two sides. Although confidence is an internal belief, it also has an external side, which concerns how assertive you *seem* in the eyes of others. This external side of confidence is the most consequential because it is often mistaken for real competence.

To go back to our opening example, while Ryan seems more confident than Shilpa, we don't know how confident he *feels*. Perhaps his displays of confidence are desperate attempts to mask his raging insecurity. When clients ask him a question, he never admits he doesn't know, out of a fear of looking stupid. Shilpa, on the other hand, may internally be more confident than Ryan—perhaps she's secure enough in herself to admit when she doesn't have all the information. But to the outside world, it looks as though Shilpa is the uncertain one.

The bottom line: regardless of how confident we feel internally, when we come across as confident to others, they will often assume that we are competent, at least until we prove them wrong.

This link between perceived confidence and competence is important. Although women are assumed to be less confident than men and some studies have shown that women appear to be less confident, a closer look at the research shows that women are internally confident. In fact, men and women are both overconfident—even if men are still more overconfident than women.

As Harvard Business School's Robin Ely and Georgetown's Catherine Tinsley write in the *Harvard Business Review*, the idea that women lack confidence is a "fallacy":

> *That assertion is commonly invoked to explain why women speak up less in meetings and do not put themselves forward for promotions unless they are 100% certain they meet all the job requirements. But research does not corroborate the idea that women are less confident than men. Analyzing more than 200 studies, Kristen Kling and colleagues concluded that the only noticeable differences occurred during adolescence; starting at age 23, differences become negligible.*[20]

A team of European academics studied hundreds of engineers and replicated Kling's finding, reporting that women do feel confident in general.[21] But the researchers also noted that women's confidence wasn't always recognized by others. Although both women and men reported feeling confident, men were much more likely to be rated by other people as appearing confident. Women's self-reports of confidence had no correlation with how others saw their confidence.

To make matters worse, for the female engineers, appearing confident had no leadership benefits at all. For the men, seeming confident translated into having influence, but for women, appearing confident did not have the same effect. To have any impact in the organization, the women had to be seen as confident, competent, and caring; all three traits were inseparable. For men, confidence alone translated into greater organizational clout, whereas a caring attitude had no effect on people's perception of leadership potential.

We are, it seems, less likely to tolerate high confidence in women than we are in men. This bias creates a lose-lose situation for women.[22] Since women are seen as less confident than men and since we see confidence as pivotal to leadership, we demand extra displays of confidence in women to consider them worthy of leadership positions. However, when a woman does seem as confident as, or more confident than, men, we are put off by her because high confidence does not fit our gender stereotypes.

If women don't lack confidence, then why do we see differences in how men and women behave? Why are women less likely to apply to jobs or to request a promotion unless they're 100 percent qualified? Why else would women speak less in meetings and be more likely to hedge their bets when making recommendations?

If the answer is not how women feel internally, it must be how they are perceived externally. In other words, differences in behavior arise not because of differences in how men and women *are*, but in how men and women *are treated*. This is what the evidence shows: women are less likely to get useful feedback, their mistakes are judged more harshly and remembered longer, their behavior is scrutinized more carefully, and their colleagues are less likely to share vital information with them. When women speak, they're more likely to be interrupted or ignored.[23]

In this context, it makes sense that even an extremely confident women would behave differently from a man. As Ely and Tinsley observed at a biotech company, the female research scientists were far less likely to speak up in meetings, even though in one-on-one interactions, they shared a lot of useful information. Leaders attributed this difference to a lack of confidence: "What these leaders had failed to see was that when women did speak in meetings, their ideas tended to be either ignored until a man restated them or shot down quickly if they contained even the slightest flaw. In contrast, when men's ideas were flawed, the meritorious elements were salvaged. Women therefore felt they needed to be 110 percent sure of their ideas before they would venture to share them. In a context in which being smart was the coin of the realm, it seemed better to remain silent than to have one's ideas repeatedly dismissed." Thus, because we choose leaders by how confident they appear rather than by how confident or competent they are, we not only end up choosing more men to lead us but ultimately choose more-incompetent men.

The dangers of overconfidence

As we've seen, the tendency to overrate our abilities and be more confident than we should applies to both men and women—remember the driving example? Both men and women rated themselves as above average. But men do this much more frequently than women do. In that poll of drivers, for example, men were 11 percentage points more overconfident than women.[24]

Another example comes from a 2012 study led by Columbia University's Ernesto Reuben and colleagues. Again, both male and female participants in the study overestimated their abilities on a math task, but men overestimated their abilities by about 30 percent, whereas women only overrated themselves by 15 percent.[25] In an ingenious follow-up study, the researchers divided the participants into teams that would compete to solve a math problem. Each team had to elect a leader to represent them; since there was a cash prize for the winning team, it was in each team's interest to select the most competent representative. But Reuben and colleagues changed the rules for some of the teams. In these teams, the chosen representative would be paid a bonus just for serving in that leadership role. As we would expect, both men and women in these teams exaggerated their abilities in an effort to win the leadership role and the bonus. But men exaggerated their abilities far more than women did and were chosen as leaders more often. As the researchers found, women were selected as leaders 30 percent less often than their competence level would predict.

As noted earlier, even if overconfidence pays off for the individual, it seldom pays off for the person's subordinates. Despite the accuracy of this observation, our love for confident people often leads us to the misguided conclusion that high confidence is advantageous per se.

Why are men more likely to be overconfident? While some kind of deep-seated evolutionary adaptation might have produced this gender difference, the simplest explanation is that men are more likely to live in a world in which their flaws are forgiven and their strengths magnified. Thus, it is harder for them to see themselves accurately. Overconfidence is the natural result of privilege.

Although there are some benefits to overconfidence in a leader—as we've seen, it can produce some self-fulfilling effects, making others believe that the leader is as good as he or she thinks—the downsides are enormous, particularly for others. Consider David Cameron. The former British prime minister's overconfident decision to call for a referendum on the country's European Union membership has led to Brexit and jeopardized not only the future of the United Kingdom but also that of Europe. And sadly—for both him and his country—the referendum was really a silly lapse. Cameron had been performing well as prime minister, with relatively high approval ratings even among his natural critics. With a strong economy and a positive reputation, Cameron thought he could silence the anti-European members of Parliament in his party by agreeing to a national referendum on the United Kingdom's EU membership. As a strong pro-Europe figure, he was clearly confident that the referendum would go his way, underestimating the probability—and the consequences—of a negative result. Fast-forward two years, and his political career is finished, with his country still experiencing huge uncertainty and in total damage-control mode.

Overconfident decisions that lead to bad results are, of course, nothing new, as evidenced by countless catastrophic leadership mistakes, including Napoleon's march on Moscow, John F. Kennedy's Bay of Pigs invasion, and the Vietnam War. By the same token, overconfident leaders routinely put themselves forward for tasks for which they are not qualified or equipped, and their lack of competence seriously handicaps the performance—and morale—of their teams.[26]

One reason overconfident leaders are more prone to reckless decisions is that they are immune to negative feedback. Most people already find it hard to digest criticism, and most organizations and societies encourage a civil environment where white lies are preferred to painful truths. For every Uber, Amazon, and Bridgewater— these and a handful of other firms that have put in place brutally honest cultures where "radical transparency" is the norm—thousands of companies believe that telling the truth is not just politically unwise but also career suicide. There is even a recent trend to eliminate negative comments from the performance review, with companies like VMware (Dell's cloud computing division), the e-commerce platform Wayfair, and Boston Consulting Group all reportedly shifting toward purely positive feedback.[27] This trend turns the performance review into a futile exercise of ingratiation where the best that employees can hope for is the ability to read between the lines to gauge what their managers want from them.

To make matters worse, leaders are even more deprived of negative feedback than employees are. The more successful and powerful you are, the more that people will suck up to you—even when they think poorly of you. Leaders must therefore be unusually self-critical and humble to anticipate potential criticisms and aspire to do better. Research shows that the most accurate criticism would come from a leader's direct reports, because they have the closest knowledge of the leader's performance. But how many employees would feel free to regularly criticize their boss? Very few, and they probably work for an exceptionally good leader if they feel free to criticize him or her. However, since most leaders—in particular, men—are overconfident about their performance, it would be naive to expect them to accept negative feedback or criticism, especially from their reports.[28]

Conversely, individuals who are aware of their weaknesses and have a realistic sense of their limitations could tune in to their subordinates and understand what they need to do to improve, but they would first need to become leaders! In an environment that selects leaders for overconfidence, people who are overly self-critical—perhaps even a tad insecure—should be in high demand, but they are more likely to be ignored or ridiculed, on the assumption that they are not sufficiently strong or secure to lead. Anyone who has ever coached a leader knows that the most coachable people are unlikely to think of themselves as better than they actually are.

And despite the common perception that confidence is a highly desirable quality, it is desirable only if it is accom-panied by actual competence. As both Dizzy Dean and the great Mohammed Ali have said, "It ain't bragging if you can back it up." People will generally celebrate your confidence, unless they believe that it is not based on real competence, or that you think more highly of yourself than you should. Think of any person you ever disliked because he or she seemed arrogant. The problem was not a lack of confidence, but rather too much of it relative to the person's actual abilities.

Unfortunately, for most organizations—unlike in sports or the military—there is little objective data to evaluate the performance of leaders. When you cannot adequately judge competence, it is hard to recognize overconfidence, and the incompetence it masks.

CHAPTER 3

Why Bad Guys Win

"He is a dreadful manager," said a worker. "I have found it impossible to work for him . . . Very often, when told a new idea, he will immediately attack it and say it is worthless or even stupid, and tell you that it was a waste of time to work on it. This alone is bad management, but if the idea is a good one he will soon be telling people about it as though it was his own."

Few people would like the idea of working for such a boss. And even fewer would expect a boss like that to be held up as one of the best business leaders of all time. But remarkably, the quote describes none other than Steve Jobs, the founder of one of the most successful companies in history.[1] (The quote comes from Jef Raskin, who led the design of the original Mac computer.) Apple has just become the first trillion-dollar company in US history, even though it has not released a blockbuster product since Jobs's death in 2011.

The Jobs paradox kept many commentators puzzled, in part because it fits with a familiar archetype: the exacting, visionary perfectionist who is turbocharged by the unstoppable force of a gargantuan ego. With his dramatic product unveilings, his stark uniform of black turtlenecks, and his megalomaniac mission, Jobs seemed to present a model for ambitious leaders to follow. It has even been said that he was capable of creating a cultish reality distortion when he talked about Apple products, convincing employees, investors, and suppliers that anything was possible. As we do with many tormented artists, we tend to see Jobs's personality quirks as inseparable from his genius.

In reality, few leaders succeed when they are as difficult and badly behaved as Jobs was. A self-made billionaire with a flawed personality succeeds *despite* his or her character defects, not because of them. What makes the Jobs story a true exception is not only that he was hired back as Apple CEO—after being fired from his own company—but also that he achieved such extraordinary levels of success. As much as his fans would like to attribute Jobs's unrivaled success to his eccentric and uncompromising personality, many narcissistic leaders have no problem distorting reality or coming up with colossal ideas or megalomaniac visions for the future. Their main problem is that they are not Steve Jobs, and without his talents, their delusions of grandeur will never become the next Apple.

We have, alas, a tendency to generalize from unrepresentative examples, mostly because they are so memorable. Einstein's lack of brilliance in his early years at school does not imply that bad grades will help you win a Nobel prize. Likewise, John Coltrane's musical genius did not result from his heroin addiction—his talent somehow managed to survive the heroin. The only advantage of a difficult personality is that it may make a person unfit for traditional employment and can consequently propel them to launch their own business out of sheer necessity, if not revenge. But there is a big gap between being a mega-successful entrepreneur and being unemployable, and that gap is a function of talent rather than personality.

Many obnoxious leaders manage not only to remain employed but also to attain impressive levels of personal career success, despite their toxic personalities. To this end, this chapter explores the relationship between leadership and the two best-known examples of such toxic traits: narcissism and psychopathy. Looking at these two character traits will allow us to examine problematic leadership in more depth than we could by just talking about difficult bosses in general. The chapter will also present an evidence-based framework for making sense of the problem.

To be sure, there is much more to the dark side of leadership than narcissism and psychopathy. So why focus on these two traits? We'll do so for a few reasons. Not only are both traits more common among leaders than in the normal population, but they also perfectly illustrate the ambivalence of the dark side. These counterproductive and undesirable tendencies coexist with—and are largely masked by—seemingly attractive traits. Narcissism and

psychopathy are so fascinating because they can simultaneously help individual leaders advance their careers while
hurting the people and organizations they lead. These
leaders are not always incompetent, but they are generally
destructive, particularly in the long run.

Various studies put the rate of psychopathy in senior
management roles at anywhere between 4 percent and
20 percent. Even at the lower end, that's four times higher
than the general population rate, which is just 1 percent.
Likewise, the prevalence of narcissism in the overall population is only 1 percent, yet studies suggest that among
CEOs, the figure is 5 percent.[2]

Both traits are also more likely to be found in men than
in women. For instance, the rate of clinical narcissism is
almost 40 percent higher in men than in women—perhaps
helping to account for men's higher rates of overconfidence,
as discussed in chapter 2. Meanwhile psychopathy occurs
three times more often in men than it does in women.

Spotting narcissism at work

What do we mean when we say that someone is narcissistic?[3]
Primarily, narcissism involves an unrealistic sense of grandiosity and superiority, manifested in the form of vanity,
self-admiration, and delusions of talent. Yet underlying
this apparent superiority complex is often an unstable self-
concept: because narcissists' self-esteem is high but fragile,
they often crave validation and recognition from others.

This craving is hardly surprising: if you are constantly showing off, you are probably desperate for others' admiration. Such inner insecurity is rarely found in naturally humble people.

Second, narcissists tend to be self-centered. They are less interested in others and have deficits in empathy, the ability to feel what others are feeling. For this reason, narcissists are rarely found displaying any genuine consideration for people other than themselves.

A third defining feature of narcissism concerns high levels of entitlement. Narcissists commonly behave as if they deserve certain privileges or enjoy higher status than their peers enjoy. Examples abound: "Do I really need to apply for a promotion?" "Why didn't I get a bigger bonus?" "Do I have to wait in line?" Such entitlements may justify narcissists' exploitative behaviors at work and elsewhere. When you think you are better than others, you perceive unfairness where there is none and behave in demeaning and condescending ways toward people.

For decades, psychologists have devised and tested different tools for detecting narcissism. The most common method is self-report questionnaires, which simply provide respondents with a list of statements relating to their personal habits, preferences, or dispositions. Examples of these statements are "I am a natural leader" and "I am more talented than most of the people I know." And if you think that this method is too transparent to work, you are wrong. A recent study led by Sara Konrath of Indiana University showed that you can spot whether someone is a narcissist with a single question: "To what extent do you agree with this statement: 'I am a narcissist.' Note: The word 'narcissist' means egotistical, self-focused, and vain."[4]

Participants then answered the question on a scale of 1 (not very true of me) to 7 (very true of me). To the researchers' surprise, narcissistic individuals were quite happy to confess to being narcissistic, and the single question captured people's narcissism with an accuracy comparable to longer, well-established tests, which the researchers demonstrated in eleven studies. Narcissism was easily detected by the single question because narcissists are not only aware of their extraordinary self-love, but also proud of it, for they truly love loving themselves, unashamedly.

Nonetheless, various less transparent methods are also available to detect narcissism. For example, executives' narcissism can be inferred from the size and attractiveness of their corporate profile picture, the number of times they are mentioned in their organizations' brochures and press releases, and the frequency with which they use the word *I* and other self-referential pronouns.[5]

For CEOs, their narcissism can also be inferred from their compensation: the bigger their egos, the bigger the gap between their salaries and those of everyone else in their organizations![6] More recently, several studies have shown that you can detect narcissism from a person's digital footprint. For example, sexier, more attractive, self-promoting Facebook pictures and, of course, an excess of selfies, all suggest narcissism.[7]

Why narcissists are more likely to become leaders

Unsurprisingly to anybody who ever opened a newspaper, narcissistic people are often leaders, and it is easy to understand why we are somehow drawn to them. Although the exact number of narcissists in leadership roles is hard to estimate—mostly because very few have their narcissism tested—several studies suggest that narcissists disproportionately occupy the leadership ranks. One study even estimated the narcissism of US presidents and concluded that on some of the key dimensions of narcissism, such as grandiosity, 80 percent of the overall population would score lower on narcissism than would the average US president.[8] To wit, who would even dream of becoming the president of the United States without feeling a sense of grandiosity? Other studies show that a person's narcissism score predicts whether he or she becomes a leader, even after controlling for gender, self-esteem, and major personality traits such as extraversion or curiosity.[9] Along the same lines, in lab experiments with leaderless groups of a few individuals with no previous knowledge of each other, narcissists emerge more frequently as leaders. Why?

First, narcissists have, or are perceived to have, some positive qualities, such as higher levels of creativity. But in reality, narcissistic people are no more creative than others are; they are just better at selling their ideas to others.

What's more, narcissists spend much more time and energy worrying about how they look. They are masters of impression management, and they seduce people by coming across as attractive and confident (the latter of which, as discussed in chapter 2, is often mistaken for competence). Impression management is a key skill for getting ahead at work, regardless of whether you're a narcissist or not.[10] But because narcissists put more time and effort into perfecting this skill than does the rest of the world, they naturally end up being better at it.

Perhaps as a result, many organizations regard their narcissistic leaders and employees as central members of their firms. Narcissists, of course, agree with this role, though they often feel more important than their firms. More than once, I have heard executives complain that their talents are not fully appreciated by their organizations while also assuring me that their own personal brand is bigger than their firm's—a classic narcissistic statement.

Being naturally more status oriented, narcissists value power and achievement more than others do. In fact, the best narcissism tests evaluate a facet called leadership or authority. Narcissism increases with people's interest in leadership and power. One of the best single statements to evaluate this aspect of narcissism is "I have a natural talent for influencing people." What better way can someone find to demonstrate his or her self-perceived superiority than to become a leader or boss? Unsurprisingly, narcissists have little interest in conventional jobs, and that includes being an employee.

Importantly, the rules of the game tend to motivate narcissists to climb up the organizational ladder. There is no better explanation for the fact that narcissists are overrepresented in the leadership ranks of organizations, and not just in corporate America.

One thing is certain: if your strategy for attracting people into leadership roles is to offer lucrative compensation packages, bestow fancy titles, and celebrate leadership as the benchmark of individual career success, you will inevitably end up with many narcissists in charge. This result is exacerbated by organizations' tendency to glorify heroic and visionary leaders. No one can compete with narcissists when it comes to formulating and selling a game-changing, pompous vision.

Sometimes, organizations may think that there is nothing wrong with having narcissists in leadership roles. Quite clearly, narcissists' air of supreme confidence can inspire and energize followers, and research indicates that a little bit of narcissism is not just common, but also beneficial, among high-performing leaders.[11] But organizations led by narcissists face two problems: First, the benefits of narcissism disappear during difficult and complex times, which every leader should expect. Second, many leaders display much more than a little amount of narcissism. And as you may have figured, they are usually male.[12]

Why men are more likely to be narcissists
(sorry, guys, it's just science)

Just as men display higher levels of confidence and self-esteem than women do, men are also more narcissistic—an extreme version of the same phenomenon. For example, the prevalence of clinical narcissism is almost 40 percent higher in men than in women. One explanation for men's higher self-esteem is that they are generally more narcissistic. A recent meta-analysis of 355 studies and almost half a million individuals aged eight to fifty-five years indicated that the gender difference in narcissism is among the highest difference found for any psychological trait.[13]

In particular, research suggests that gender differences in narcissism are mostly driven by two specific aspects for which men score higher than women do. The first, the so-called exploitative entitlement dimension, consistently predicts whether individuals engage in behaviors that harm colleagues and the organization. These behaviors include theft, bullying, harassment, and cyber-loafing (pretending to work while really just surfing the internet). The second aspect, leadership or authority, explains why certain individuals are much more likely to regard themselves as leader-like and predicts whether leaders are likely to adopt an authoritarian and despotic style when they are in charge.

Why are men more narcissistic? Two major theories provide answers to this question. From an evolutionary standpoint, men can be expected to be more narcissistic because sexual selection favors dominance, competition, and status-seeking. From a cultural standpoint, if men have historically occupied more powerful and desirable positions in society, then it is to be expected that, as a result, they are more assertive and entitled.

We can test the validity of these theories by examining changes in narcissism rates over time. If the evolutionary theory is correct, it would predict a rather static gender difference over time—evolutionary changes tend to take thousands of years to unfold. If the cultural explanation is correct, then we would be more likely to see changes in rates of narcissism over the last few decades, as our society becomes more gender-balanced and egalitarian. In fact, we do see such changes.

Meta-analytic studies suggest that the gender differences in narcissism have indeed been declining over the past few decades, largely because women have become more narcissistic, rather than men becoming less so. This change reaffirms the danger of encouraging women to lean in or act more like men to climb the corporate ladder. We are only inviting them to strengthen a problematic leadership model and augment rather than reduce current incompetence rates. Fortunately, telling women to act more narcissistically won't necessarily guarantee them a seat at the table, given the still-present backlash against female leaders who act like narcissists. This behavior violates the social stereotype of women as more communal, tender, and selfless. Urging narcissism is just bad advice all around. Sadly, however, we have still not realized that traditionally feminine prosocial qualities are critical for effective leadership.

Just as problematically, men are rarely rewarded for behaving more humbly, and we have far too much tolerance for male leaders who behave like narcissists.[14] In support of this assertion, a series of studies by Timothy Judge at the University of Notre Dame and Beth Livingston from Cornell University found that men's careers tend to suffer when the men are friendly, empathetic, and agreeable. More specifically, the authors revealed a general negative association between these traits and earnings, implying that "nice guys and gals finish last," although being nice is more problematic for men.[15] Because the premium for being self-centered is therefore bigger for men than for women, the public's reaction to narcissistic leaders is generally more negative when they are female (e.g., Martha Stewart) than male (e.g., Richard Branson). Shockingly, though, there is still a payoff for both men and women who behave in undesirable ways.

Why narcissists don't make good leaders

A caveat at the outset: leadership effectiveness stems from many personal qualities (and is constrained by situational issues). Narcissism can easily coexist with other talents. If you're a narcissist or you work for one, you should know that narcissist leaders might nonetheless have a positive impact on their followers and organizations.

Take Elon Musk, by any measure an exceptionally successful man. Having cofounded and sold PayPal, he quickly moved on to launching a range of ventures with world-changing aspirations for how we generate energy, transport ourselves and our goods, interface with machines, and explore our solar system. These ventures are unified in their vision—an obsessive quest—for a more sustainable and resilient future for humanity and are executed through a mixture of brilliant engineering and out-of-the-box thinking. To be sure, the ultimate success of these endeavors remains an open question, but so far, they have defied expectations and inspired millions.

Musk's talent for entrepreneurship, defined as the ability to translate original and useful ideas into practical innovations, is undeniably outstanding. And yet, his reputation also has a narcissistic side, which has been recently manifested—rather often—in his combative rants with investors, the media, and employees, his confrontational and erratic social media presence, and his inability to accept criticism calmly and maturely. This pattern of behavior— and I'm only referring to his public persona rather than implying he may be a narcissist or making a clinical diagnosis—stands in stark contrast to the humanistic nature of his vision for positive change. The behavior undermines his brilliant bright side and has led a *New York Times* op-ed columnist to describe Musk as the Donald Trump of Silicon Valley.

Of course, there is a long history of successful entrepreneurs, industrialists, and self-made billionaires who stood out as much for their talents and achievements as for their eccentric, difficult, and volatile public images. Howard Hughes spent most of his later life in complete isolation rather than having to engage with the public and be exposed to the germs he so feared. John Paul Getty installed a coin-operated pay phone in his villa to avoid subsidizing his guests' phone calls. Timothy Armstrong, CEO of AOL, fired an executive on a live conference call after the executive snapped a photo of Armstrong for the internal website. And we have already mentioned Jobs, the most famous example, earlier in this chapter.

In short, narcissistic tendencies are more likely to get in your way, as a leader, than they are to help you. And they have particularly bad long-term effects on other people.

Narcissists may charm others initially, but these first impressions usually wear out in the end. For example, a recent study collected longitudinal data from 175 retail stores in the Netherlands, spanning three years.[16] The results showed that the more employees knew—and interacted with—their managers, the more negatively the employees viewed managers with higher narcissism scores. In other words, as long as bosses had limited interactions with their employees, their narcissism did not automatically translate into a negative reputation. However, it was far more unlikely that narcissists maintained a good image with employees after prolonged interactions with them. These results are consistent with much research showing that it can be particularly difficult for narcissists to maintain long-term relationships.

Anyone thinking of emulating Steve Jobs to become the next superstar entrepreneur will likely be deemed unemployable rather than a business genius. The fact that Jobs was fired from his own company is not unusual. It happens to many entrepreneurs, often because the very people who feel compelled to start their own businesses are the same people who find it difficult to work well in other people's businesses.

In any event, the key question is not what effect narcissism has on the leaders themselves but how it affects everyone else. And in this regard, the research evidence is most compelling, suggesting that organizations are much better off minimizing the number of narcissists in leadership roles. There are three big reasons for this recommendation.

First, narcissists are significantly more prone to counterproductive and antisocial work behaviors, such as bullying, fraud, white-collar crime, and harassment, including sexual harassment. And, given the contagious nature of these toxic behaviors, their teams and organizations are more likely to engage in these unethical and destructive activities as well.[17]

This research predates the recent explosion of harassment that prompted the #MeToo movement, which is just a newer symptom of the same old phenomenon: narcissistic leaders—usually men—who abuse their power to advance their own interest and end up harming not only their victims but also their organizations. Take Harvey Weinstein, the founder of Miramax studios and one of the most successful and powerful producers in Hollywood. There's no question that Weinstein is a brilliant mind, responsible for films such as *Pulp Fiction*, *Gangs of New York*, and *The Crying Game*, and he has apparently been thanked more times than God in Oscar winners' acceptance speeches. But his dark side became a matter of public discussion in October 2017, when in one month alone, eighty women came forward with sexual abuse allegations against him, including sexual harassment, assault, and rape. To be clear, not all narcissists engage in these or other criminal behaviors, but when powerful and successful leaders do, it is often because they are narcissistic.

Second, although narcissists generally perform perfectly well just after their promotion to a leadership role, this usually short honeymoon period is followed by a much bleaker phase. For instance, narcissistic leaders, especially narcissist CEOs, are paid more than their counterparts, and they are also more likely to push their organizations into extravagant acquisitions and other investments without, unfortunately, producing a higher return on investment (ROI).[18]

For all the initial appeal of their grand visions, narcissistic leaders also tend to have difficulties with execution, so they aren't likely to deliver on their big plans. Partly because self-absorption limits leaders' ability to bring others along with them, narcissists struggle to get others on board when it comes to turning ambitious plans into a concrete reality. These interpersonal deficits prevent narcissistic leaders from building and maintaining high-performing teams and organizations.

Whereas a good leader gets along with team members and peers to help them get ahead of competing teams and organizations, a narcissistic leader gets ahead within his or her own team. Such a leader becomes a lone wolf at best and a parasite at worst.

Third, even when an organization is aware of these problems, they are not easily fixed once a narcissist has been appointed to a leadership role. A person's narcissism changes little over time, so we cannot just wait for narcissistic leaders to get better. Studies have found that adult levels of narcissism can be predicted from early childhood measures, even in children as young as four years. There's also a hereditary component to narcissism much as there is for any other psychological or physical trait.[19]

Narcissistic leaders are notably less coachable, not least because of their stiff resistance to negative feedback. They're quick to blame others for their own mistakes and to take credit for others' achievements. In the unlikely event that narcissists do pay attention to criticism, they will usually respond aggressively and retaliate rather than use that feedback to improve. To make matters worse, these tendencies are exacerbated by narcissists' impulsive nature. Because of their poor self-control, narcissists have trouble sustaining any development or self-improvement initiative.

When presented with accurate critical feedback on their performance, most people can learn to inhibit counterproductive or undesirable aspects of their personality. They must be willing to do so and able to internalize that feedback to increase their self-awareness. But these attitudes and abilities are much less likely with narcissists.

Why we love psychopaths

Let us now turn our attention to the other major dark-side trait. Psychopathy is often discussed in connection with leadership, particularly when it comes to famous political and business leaders. Unlike narcissism, which is widespread, psychopathy is rare. And yet few toxic character traits have attracted as much public fascination and media attention as psychopathy has—even though only about 1 percent of the general population is thought to have psychopathic tendencies.

Perhaps part of our obsession with psychopaths stems from the disproportionate rate at which they seem to succeed. Professor Robert Hare, a pioneer in the field of criminal psychology and coauthor of the influential book *Snakes in Suits*, famously noted that "not all psychopaths are in prison; some are in the boardroom."[20] According to estimates he reports in a subsequent study, there are three times as many psychopaths in management roles than in the overall population.[21] More recently, a much higher figure of around 20 percent (one in five) has been reported for another US corporate sample.[22] This large range in variability reflects how people measure psychopathy, but psychopathy levels do increase with levels of career success.

So, what makes someone psychopathic? The first salient feature is a lack of moral inhibition, which at an extreme is manifested in the form of strong antisocial tendencies and an intense desire to break the rules, even just for the sake of doing so. And when psychopaths do break the rules, they feel no guilt or remorse to avoid a repeat of events.

People with psychopathic tendencies are also more prone to making reckless behavioral choices. For instance, psychopaths are more likely to drink, smoke, take drugs, and have promiscuous sexual relations and extramarital affairs.[23] To be clear, not all adrenaline junkies are psychopathic, but the vast majority of psychopathic individuals are thrill seekers, and their reduced concern for danger will put them and others at risk.

A third defining feature of psychopaths is their lack of empathy. They don't care about what others are thinking or feeling, despite being able to understand those feelings.[24] As a result, psychopaths are known for their cold dispositions. The absence of empathy is probably a major cause for their lack of moral constraints; it's obviously much harder to behave in prosocial ways when you don't care about people.

However, perhaps more than any other dark-side trait, psychopathy has a socially desirable side, too, which makes it irresistible and an important career weapon for individuals, especially when it is coupled with intelligence or good looks. Not that psychopathic people are necessarily more attractive or intelligent, but they are certainly much more destructive when they do have these more appealing qualities.

Some evidence suggesting a positive association between psychopathy and verbal ability explains why psychopaths are often quite eloquent and persuasive.[25] Other positive qualities associated with psychopathy include superior resilience under stress, in terms of both staying calm in the face of pressure and recovering from setbacks, and the ability to strategically channel aggressive tendencies. For instance, James Bond, despite rarely being described as psychopathic, exhibits many of the textbook features of the trait. He releases his aggression and lack of empathy by being a ruthless killer on behalf of the British government and by sleeping with his enemies' wives (on behalf of no one but himself).

Many wildly celebrated character traits, such as courage and risk-taking, often coexist with psychopathic tendencies. For example, during the last major tsunami that devastated Thailand, an Australian businessman became an instant hero with the media for singlehandedly saving the lives of twenty people, yet it later transcended that this same individual had been a fugitive of the Australian police for years because of assault and robbery charges.[26] In a similar vein, a British fireman who was awarded a medal of honor for his heroic actions during the 2005 London terrorist attack, when he risked his life saving the passengers of the bombed bus, is now serving a fourteen-year prison sentence for his involvement in a $135 million cocaine ring.[27]

An even more lethal aspect to psychopathic individuals is their tendency to come across as charming and charismatic, which, in addition to their masterful self-promotion and deception skills, explains how they manage to emerge as leaders. Indeed, charisma chiefly explains the prominence of psychopathic leaders. Not that all charismatic people are psychopaths, but a great proportion of psychopaths do display charisma, defined as the tendency to be perceived as charming, likable, and magnetic (more on charisma in the next chapter).

Although psychopathy is not exclusive to men, it is much more common in men than in women.[28] While few studies exist on gender differences in psychopathy, the evidence we do have suggests that psychopathy is three times more likely in men than in women, a difference that is already noticeable during adolescence.[29] This pattern is consistent with the higher prevalence of antisocial behaviors in males.[30] Anywhere in the world, we find many more men than women in prison, as well as many more men than women who engage in violent behaviors, harassment, cyberbullying and other bullying, overt aggression, and reckless self- and other-harming behaviors such as fatal driving accidents. All these differences between men and women should result in a natural preference for female leaders, but our inability to resist psychopaths' charm has the opposite effect.

When psychopaths lead

Alexander Nix is the founder and former CEO of Cambridge Analytica, a political consulting firm that played a significant role in determining the results of the last US presidential election and the Brexit referendum. After a meteoric rise to fame, which earned him a reputation of pioneer, maverick, and rock star of the digital marketing world, Nix was filmed by an undercover reporter as the then CEO made a sales pitch that included entrapment, bribes, and sex workers. Naturally, the media and public reacted with shock, which led to the suspension of Nix as CEO. But traits such as reckless risk-taking, greed, and a feeble sense of morality are useful if you want to illegally harvest seventy million Facebook profiles to target people with fake news to disrupt the results of major elections. The company filed for bankruptcy in May 2018, but not before Nix allegedly withdrew an $8 million golden parachute.[31]

What happens once psychopaths are in charge? How will they lead, and what effects will they have on their followers, subordinates, and organizations? Although psychopathic individuals may rise to become leaders because of their charisma, once they are in leadership roles, they are less likely to inspire or otherwise influence their subordinates. Instead, these leaders operate passively, failing to fulfill basic management tasks such as evaluating performance, giving accurate feedback, rewarding employees, and holding teams accountable for meeting goals.[32] In short, psychopathy offers few advantages to effective leadership; most psychopaths are incompetent as leaders.

Psychopathic individuals tend to have poor overall job performance, largely because of their lack of diligence, their disdain for deadlines and processes, and their failure to assume responsibilities.[33] This range of problematic work behaviors explains why psychopathic leaders are rated more negatively by both their bosses and their direct reports. Even when they are perceived as trustworthy, several red flags will predict inferior leadership performance. These red flags include the inability to build and motivate team members, an unwillingness to accept blame and responsibility, a lack of follow-through, and impulsive unpredictability.[34]

There is also robust evidence linking psychopathy to less considerate and more laissez-fair leadership styles, both of which are generally ineffective. Teams led by psychopathic individuals are significantly less engaged and, in turn, more likely to burn out and underperform.[35]

Psychopathic leaders create many of the same issues that narcissists create in their organizations. For example, a big problem with picking psychopathic individuals for leadership roles concerns their much more common antisocial and counterproductive work behaviors, such as theft, cyber-loafing, absenteeism, and bullying. A recent meta-analysis shows that psychopathic individuals are significantly more likely to engage in these and other activities that harm their peers, teams, and organizations.[36] It appears, then, that the superficial charm of psychopathic leaders, like that of narcissists, is short-lived, quickly morphing from charisma in the early stages to an off-putting and untrustworthy demeanor in the end.

Interestingly, the relationship between psychopathy and problematic work behaviors tends to weaken at higher levels of seniority. While this observation might suggest that psychopathic leaders are better able to inhibit their destructive tendencies when at the top, powerful people might simply be better able to get away with bad behavior—or not get caught.

Research also suggests that the degree of psychopathic leaders' antisocial and counterproductive behaviors may partly depend on how much these leaders identify with their organizations. When leaders feel a close connection with their firms, they behave better, and vice versa. Moreover, certain cultures elicit behaviors that are more toxic than others, and not just for psychopaths. Interestingly, toxic cultures can be regarded as the product of psychopathic leaders, because leaders tend to create cultures in their own image. In that sense, psychopathy is self-perpetuating. When psychopaths rule, they will create toxic cultures that incubate even greater numbers of psychopathic leaders, who will in turn thrive much as bacteria and parasites do in polluted or contaminated environments.

A recent study by Michael Housman from Cornerstone OnDemand and Dylan Minor at Northwestern University's Kellogg School of Management compared the economic benefits of removing toxic workers from an organization with the benefits of adding high-performing employees.[37] They mined an impressive data set comprising more than fifty thousand employees across eleven firms that represented various types of organizations and various commercial sectors. Housman and Minor looked at a wide range of bad behaviors (e.g., egregious policy violations, sexual harassment, workplace violence, and fraud).

Their analysis revealed that the average benefit of firing toxic workers is around four times greater than that of adding a good employee to the organization. Remarkably, even if companies could attract a superstar employee—defined as someone in the top 1 percent of job performance—getting rid of a toxic worker would be twice as beneficial financially. And this benefit is without considering any likely collateral damage, such as litigation, regulatory penalties, and decreases in employee morale. If the ripple effect for bad behaviors is as strong for employees, one can only imagine how big it is for leaders, who affect many more people in the organization.

Spotting psychopaths before you promote them

"He would never be the most charming person in the room," author Diana Henriques told NPR interviewer Terry Gross. "He would make you feel like you were the most charming person in the room. The magic of his personality is how easy it is to believe him—almost how much you want to believe him."[38]

Henriques was talking with Gross about Bernie Madoff, the subject of her latest book, *The Wizard of Lies*. Madoff had been one of Wall Street's most admired investors, regarded by experts as a financial maverick comparable to Warren Buffett. After a modest upbringing and lackluster education, Madoff founded a penny stock trading business with just $5,000 of capital in 1960, initially growing it through his father-in-law's connections and money. To compete with large investment firms, he pioneered the use of computer-based information dissemination, a technological innovation that would later become the basis of the NASDAQ, to which he became the nonexecutive chairman.

The rest of the story is well known: Madoff created the biggest Ponzi scheme and largest financial fraud in history, taking $65 billion from forty-eight hundred clients. In 2009, he pleaded guilty to eleven federal felonies, including securities fraud, money laundering, and theft, and was sentenced to 150 years in prison. Although the scale of Madoff's crimes is unprecedented, what is arguably more unusual for an prominent corporate leader is that he is serving time in prison, where Henriques interviewed him. People like Madoff are usually too big to fail.

Unsurprisingly for a trait once described as "the mask of sanity," psychopathy is not easily detected by laypeople.[39] For this reason, you want to be alert to the potential risks of basing hiring decisions on short-term interactions with candidates. In fact, given their deceptive nature, fearless attitude, short-term likability, and skilled impression management, you can expect psychopaths to perform quite well during job interviews.[40] Yet, just as you wouldn't marry someone after only a first date, you should not select someone for a leadership job solely because of the person's interview performance—which is exactly that, a performance.

Psychopaths are hard to detect, but you can simultaneously evaluate a leader's psychopathy and predict its effects on his or her subordinates. How? You can simply ask the leader's subordinates to rate their boss on critical indicators of psychopathy. In one study, for example, employees were asked to rate their bosses on various personality aspects, such as "can make a joke out of anyone," "enjoys being disruptive," and "is not sincere."[41]

Scientist have developed concise measures of psychopathy, such as the Short Dark Triad assessment.[42] With just fifteen self-report statements, you can get a good sense of an individual's psychopathy level. Here are some of those statements:

I am a thrill seeker.

I like to get revenge on authorities.

I never feel guilty.

People who mess with me always regret it.

Of course, test takers can certainly fake their answers by portraying themselves in a less psychopathic way and by presenting a much more prosocial and conformist aspect of their personality. But such misrepresentation doesn't happen enough to invalidate this test. Rather, people with psychopathic tendencies seem proud to answer honestly or at least are too defiant to hide their views, perhaps because they have little guilt about their personality or care little about what others make of them.

In any event, studies have also shed light on several passive measures of psychopathy, such as people's social media activity and digital footprints. With these measures, we do not need to rely exclusively on people's self-report to deduce their psychopathic inclinations. For example, a study found that the number of selfies people post on social media reliably indicates their psychopathy level.[43] Psychopathy can also be detected in language, as psychopathic individuals speak and write in a more dominant and coercive way and express more aggression and irritability.[44] For instance, the tendency to swear is a consistent indicator of higher psychopathy. Another linguistic feature associated with psychopathy is the proclivity to talk about power, money, sex, and physical needs, whereas lower-psychopathy individuals tend to talk more about family, friends, and spirituality.[45] In short, we have numerous intuitive signals to detect people with psychopathic tendencies. To paraphrase Freud, sometimes as cigar is just a cigar.

CHAPTER 4

The Charisma Myth

She wakes up every morning between 6:00 and 6:30 in her modest apartment. After checking the news, she prepares breakfast for her and her husband around 8:00. At 9:00, she heads to the office, where she meets with her team and discusses the main agenda items for the day. Meetings kick off around 9:30, and as chair, she invites her diverse team to engage in a calm and fact-based discussion, taking the role of a moderator. Next, she attends a working lunch, followed by more meetings with internal and external stakeholders. Most of her afternoon is spent preparing for her next appointments and working on some presentations. She returns home around 10:00 p.m. and is in bed my midnight.[1]

For leading the fourth-biggest economy in the world, Angela Merkel lives an unremarkable life. And unlike most of the world's political leaders, there is little excitement or controversy about her, let alone scandals. Despite her reputation as the most competent head of state of recent times and as the de facto leader of the European Union, there will probably be no movies made about Merkel, who by 2017 had been elected German chancellor four consecutive times.

Like Merkel, the most effective business leaders in the world are not exactly known for their charisma. But we have trouble paying attention to them or remembering them, precisely because they are so discrete. It is much easier for us to focus on and remember the superloud leaders who excel at, well, drawing attention to themselves! Jim Collins, an influential management consultant, provided conclusive evidence in support of this argument. He carefully scrutinized the characteristics of CEOs from companies that had substantially outperformed their industry and market rivals for the past years. His analysis showed that the most effective CEOs were not charismatic but were remarkably persistent and humble. They excelled not at self-promotion but at nurturing talent in their teams. Instead of aspiring to a possible second career as standup comedians or reality TV stars, these effective leaders worked to make *other* people shine and especially get people working together as a high-performing team. Although such leaders are underrepresented in our collective memory and online—just google "humble leader" image to see how many figures you recognize—there are obviously many real-life examples that we ought to remember.

Let's consider several executives who perfectly illustrate Collins's profile of quiet, humble leaders, most of whom you may not have heard of. Like Merkel, these leaders are unlikely to be the subject of a Hollywood movie anytime soon.

Amancio Ortega, the founder and chairman of the Zara fashion empire and the richest person in Europe, seldom speaks in public or accepts awards. In a rare article about him, the *Economist* noted that "so few photos existed of him pre-flotation that investors who visited awkwardly confused him with other staff."[2]

IKEA founder Ingvar Kamprad was reportedly worth $25 billion just before his death in 2018. But he lived in a modest house, drove a 1993 Volvo, bought his clothes at a flea market, and never traveled first class.[3]

Mary Barra is the CEO of General Motors, where she started at the age of eighteen. Despite being the most powerful female executive in the world and the first female CEO of any car company, she is consensus driven and team oriented, and her personality has been described as "vanilla" and "quiet."[4] According to Joann Muller of *Forbes*, Wall Street hailed Barra for accomplishing more in three years than most CEOs do in thirty; under her leadership, General Motors has enjoyed three years of record earnings.[5]

Zhou Qunfei, the founder of Lens Technology, which manufactures smartphone screens—probably yours, if you have an Apple or a Samsung phone—is the richest self-made woman in the world, as well as the richest woman in China. Zhou grew up in a poor farming family in rural China and dropped out of school at sixteen to start working in a factory, where she saved enough money to start her own business. Despite her extraordinary accomplishments, she is notoriously media shy and credits her success to hard work and a relentless desire to learn, a rather more silent— and critical—quality than charisma.

The effects of humble leadership tend to cascade down to the rest of the organization, turning leaders into genuine role models. These effects have been demonstrated in recent studies by Brad Owens from the Marriott School of Business at Brigham Young University and David Hekman from the Leeds School of Business at the University of Colorado. When leaders behave humbly, employees emulate this behavior and display more modesty, admit mistakes, share credit with others, and are more receptive to others' ideas and feedback. Using data from 607 individuals grouped into 161 teams (both in research labs and in real work environments), the authors demonstrated a social-contagion effect for humble leadership, which enhanced selfless and collaborative behaviors in their followers and, in turn, in team performance.[6]

The charisma allure

Margarita Mayo, a researcher at IE Business School in Madrid, describes the conflict between humility and charisma: "The research is clear: when we choose humble, unassuming people as our leaders, the world around us becomes a better place . . . Yet instead of following the lead of these unsung heroes, we appear hardwired to search for superheroes: over-glorifying leaders who exude charisma."[7] This preference for charismatic leaders especially applies in times of crisis. Mayo's own research shows that when followers are feeling anxious, they're not only more likely to choose charismatic leaders, but also more likely to perceive charisma in the leaders they have already chosen.

Mayo's observations point to an important aspect of charisma: it exists in the eye of the beholder. Charisma therefore differs from narcissism and psychopathy, which are personality traits with a known biological basis; charisma is merely an inference that followers make about their leader. In fact, you cannot measure charisma other than through others' perceptions of it. Sure, some people will tell you they have charisma (and they may well believe it), but their own views by no means indicate their actual charisma.

Despite the insignificance of charisma with regards to leadership effectiveness, you can ask anyone about the fundamental qualities of a leader and he or she will inevitably list charisma among the top traits. The association is so strong that people will struggle to come up with a single example of a famous leader who is *not* charismatic.

A team led by Mansour Javidan, at the Thunderbird School of Global Management, Arizona State University, explored cross-cultural differences in people's perceptions of leadership talent across sixty-two countries. The team grouped the countries into ten cultural clusters: Anglo, Confucian Asia, Eastern Europe, Germanic Europe, Latin America, Latin Europe, Middle East, Nordic Europe,

Southern Asia, and sub-Saharan Africa. Although the relevance of most leadership traits, such as status-seeking, risk-taking, and competitiveness, varied considerably from one culture to the next, charisma was universally viewed as a key ingredient of leadership talent.[8]

Moreover, it takes us just a few seconds to "establish" that someone has charisma. Much recent research has decoded how impressions of charisma are formed, why we come to perceive people as charismatic, and what those perceptions—or attributions—mean.

Konstantin Tskhay and his colleagues at the University of Toronto, for example, recently set out to explore these issues. They showed 1,307 participants short video clips of different actors who were unknown to the participants. The actors were asked to read a random political speech as persuasively as possible for five minutes. The experimenters then removed the audio, experimentally manipulated the length of the clips, and examined how actor characteristics such as their attractiveness, eye contact, and whether they wore eyeglasses influenced the participants' attributions of their charisma.

Tskhay's group found that participants took a mere five seconds to decide whether someone was charismatic and that longer exposure to the actors did not alter those initial impressions. Actors who were more physically attractive, who made more eye contact, and who were white, were deemed more charismatic.[9]

Whatever charisma may mean to people, and regardless of how accurate instant perceptions of it are, charisma is self-fulfilling, as there are real consequences to seeing someone as charismatic, in particular if they are a leader. In that sense, charisma is sometimes equated to love at first sight: it is hypnotic and energizing and needs no explanation. Thus charisma is so indefinable that when we try to make sense of it, we will most likely end up rationalizing it or justifying our feelings instead of coming up with an objective interpretation of the leader's ability.

People will passionately defend the qualities of leaders they deem charismatic, just as they would blindly defend a person they are in love with: with no concern for facts or objective evidence in support of their views. Unfortunately, the same biases at play when people decide that someone is charismatic or a potential leader come into play when they have to evaluate that person's leadership performance later on.

Indeed, charisma clouds people's evaluations of how leaders actually perform—not just their leadership potential. Rather than being objective, we are less judgmental about leaders' performance when we see them as charismatic, and we are more critical when we don't. To use a recent example: how charismatic you find Hillary Clinton or Donald Trump better predicts your evaluation of their performance than does how the two politicians actually perform. Why? Our desire to understand reality is not as strong as our desire to think highly of ourselves. Consequently, if we acknowledge that a leader whom we see as charismatic is performing poorly, then we are admitting that we are a poor judge of character.[10] Charismatic leaders are therefore often evaluated more favorably by their bosses and subordinates and are promoted more often than noncharismatic leaders. Moreover, teams with charismatic leaders often have higher levels of job satisfaction and, in turn, performance: if you like and admire the person you work for, even if the picture you have is just an illusion, you will no doubt be more motivated to impress the person by working hard.[11] And charismatic individuals will generally reciprocate this relationship by managing down rather than up, so they tend to focus more on pleasing their subordinates than sucking up to their bosses.[12]

Women and the charisma dilemma

A Google image search for "famous leaders" generates almost only charismatic leaders: Barack Obama, Mahatma Gandhi, Martin Luther King, Richard Branson, Steve Jobs, and so on. This quick and simple way to access the collective archetype of leadership also highlights how charisma is a gendered trait: the only women who appear in the first page are Margaret Thatcher and Mother Teresa.

Although academic research on gender and charisma is relatively scant, an important disadvantage for women when it comes to charisma is that perceptions of charisma are often a consequence rather than a cause of leadership success. So, while we may attribute leadership skills to people who seem charismatic, we are even more likely to attribute charisma to people who have succeeded as leaders.

Naturally, women have more difficulty demonstrating their potential for leadership when they are not considered for leadership positions in the first place, and a self-fulfilling prophecy ensues.

For example, research shows that leaders who occupy a more central position in their organizations' networks—meaning they have more connections—are more likely to be seen as charismatic. They gain a reputation for being charismatic if they forge more relationships within their companies.[13]

Unfortunately, since women are underrepresented in the leadership ranks, fewer of them occupy a central position in their organizations' networks. They therefore often end up being perceived as tokens in gender-diversity programs. Likewise, leadership experts Rob Kaiser and Wanda Wallace suggest that since women are less likely to occupy strategic leadership roles, they are rated lower on strategic leadership ability.[14] In contrast, women are generally rated higher on operational leadership skills, which are more central to the role of managers, and lower on charisma. Women face an apparent chicken-and-egg situation: because they rarely hold senior leadership roles, we are less prone to see them as charismatic, and because we don't see them as charismatic, we assume that they are not good leaders.

And yet, when researchers measure charismatic leadership using robust tools, going beyond whatever confusing and vague attribution laypeople may make of it and asking employees to judge their leaders after extended interactions, women score higher on measures of charismatic leadership. A study by Kevin Groves from California State University took a close look at how employees evaluate their leaders on critical markers of charisma, focusing not on first impressions but on the leaders' long-term reputation.[15] A total of 108 senior leaders from various organizations across many industries and sectors were rated by 325 of their direct reports. Groves asked employees to complete a scientifically validated measure of charismatic leadership, one that predicts positive organizational outcomes, such as team performance, revenues, profits, and high employee engagement. The key indicators of charisma included the following behaviors:

- Inspires employees, communicates, and implements the vision well

- Acts as a role model and *walks the talk*

- Is sensitive to the cultural norms of the organizations

- Recognizes employees for their accomplishments, giving credit where it is due

- Uses emotional communication effectively

- Is good at identifying and nurturing employees' potential

- In addition, the leaders also completed assessments of their own social and emotional skills.

This study had two important differences from the studies on social perception discussed earlier. First, because the Groves study made no direct mention of charisma, it helped minimize biases and confusion around what the term actually means. Second, employees have plentiful data to answer these questions. We are not talking about five seconds here, but are talking about months of working for someone. Predictably, there was great alignment among employees rating the same leader—they all seemed to describe the same person. The results showed that employees rated their female bosses higher on most of the above-listed behaviors and that this difference was a function of women's stronger social and emotional skills (more on this in the next chapter).

In another study, Herminia Ibarra and Otilia Obodaru at INSEAD examined thousands of 360-degree assessments (i.e., feedback from the leaders' various coworkers, including subordinates, peers, and bosses) of leaders who had participated in their executive education programs.[16] In line with previous evidence on gender stereotypes and bias, the researchers expected to find that women were rated lower than men. But instead, their results revealed the opposite: as they wrote in a 2009 *Harvard Business Review* article, "as a group, women outshone men in most of the leadership dimensions measured." In fact, in only one of the ten leadership skills assessed—envisioning—did men receive higher ratings. The men received these higher scores only when the raters themselves were men—more specifically, male peers, the very people likely to be competing with the women for the next promotion. On all the other nine skills, both men and women rated female leaders higher, and female leaders rated women higher on envisioning. Male subordinates and male supervisors rated men and women roughly equally on vision.

The dark side of charisma

No doubt, charisma can be a helpful tool for leaders, enabling them to build and maintain connections with others and to persuade people that they must follow a specific course of action. After all, "a leader is a dealer in hope," as Napoleon famously remarked.

In one of the most fascinating studies on this issue, Ronald Deluga from Bryant University carried out a historical analysis of thirty-nine US presidents, from George Washington to Ronald Reagan. Deluga's aimed to explore the degree to which the presidents' charisma, narcissism, and leadership performance overlapped. To assess their charisma and leadership style, Deluga showed anonymized biographical extracts from the presidents to various independent raters, who judged the now-anonymous men on specific indicators of charisma, for example, "keeps in contact with the American public and its moods," "uses rhetoric effectively," and "is a dynamo of energy and determination." Another set of raters were used to evaluate the presidents on key dimensions of narcissism, such as vanity, entitlement, and superiority, picking from paired statements the option that best represented each president. For example, the raters chose between "believes he/she is much like everybody else" and "believes he/she is an extraordinary person." To assess the presidents' performance, Deluga used expert ratings from a range of American historians who looked at factors such as general prestige, strength of action, presidential activeness, war activity, and administrative accomplishments.

To illustrate the strong connection between charisma, narcissism, and performance, Deluga used the example of Franklin D. Roosevelt, one of the top scorers on all three traits: "He was supremely ebullient and self-confident. He possessed a persuasive and vibrant golden voice and displayed remarkable gifts for leadership in times of crisis. Also, Roosevelt maintained an image of superiority and the absolute assurance as to the value and importance of what he was doing. Even among his ardent supporters, a common complaint about Roosevelt was his devious and deceptive nature; he never spoke with total candidness to anyone."[17]

Charismatic leaders excel at giving people hope; there are no better vehicles than charisma for selling a vision or providing individuals with meaning. However, when leaders are incompetent or unethical, the power of charisma will be turned against their followers, mobilizing them toward counterproductive or even self-destructive goals. As Allen Grabo, an evolutionary psychologist at the University of Amsterdam, and his colleagues note, "charismatic signals are often deliberately hijacked by individual leaders who fail to bring benefits to followers, but instead benefit themselves . . . individuals who come across at first glance as charming or inspiring, but who have no ability or willingness to provide coordination benefits."[18]

As illustrated in chapter 3, psychopathic and narcissistic leaders are often perceived as charismatic, and their followers can be blind to their toxicity. To be clear, many charismatic people are neither psychopathic nor narcissistic, in the same way that many psychopathic and narcissistic people have absolutely no charisma. But when these dark-side traits are lubricated with charisma, they can make leaders pretty lethal. The more we rely on charisma as a marker of leadership potential, the more we risk ending up with toxic leaders who are exploiting their charms and influence to grab power and manipulate their followers.

If there is one important leadership lesson in history, it is that in the hands of immoral and selfish leaders, charisma is a very powerful deception tool to enlist followers' support for malignant causes. Adolph Hitler, Joseph Stalin, Mao Zedong, and Benito Mussolini were all charismatic, and the same applies to most dictators successful in creating a personality cult around their charisma. But such leaders would have caused far less damage if they had been less charismatic. By the same token, a less charismatic Osama bin Laden would have had a harder time persuading people to crash a plane into the twin towers, and Jonestown would have been less likely to happen had Jim Jones been less charismatic. This dark side of charisma can still be observed at far less extreme levels of problematic leadership. For example, charisma helps US presidents maintain higher approval ratings even when they are not performing well. People will be more likely to tolerate a bad president who is charismatic than they would tolerate a high-performing president who is not.[19]

Even when leaders are competent and ethical, the effects of charisma on leadership performance are more mixed than previously assumed. A team led by Jasmine Vergauwe from the Ghent University demonstrated these mixed effects. The authors analyzed data from three independent studies, involving global samples of eight hundred business leaders and around seventy-five hundred of their superiors, peers, and subordinates. The leaders' seniority ranged from first-line supervisors all the way up to the C-suite. The results showed that charismatic leaders were good at strategic tasks, such as formulating and selling a vision, setting the direction for the organization, and pushing for innovation. However, they were bad at tactical aspects of leadership, such as efficiency, execution, and organizing. Vergauwe and her colleagues concluded that the too-much-of-a-good-thing effect also applies to charisma and that if organizations want an all-round performance in leaders, they would be well advised to hire people with a moderate amount of charisma. Such a balanced dose of this characteristic would make leaders versatile enough to be both strategic and operational.

Thus, even if charisma may render leaders more influential, paying too much attention to it will lead us to ignore other, more important leadership signals, such as competence, integrity, and self-awareness. Because of the abstract nature of leadership, charisma often ends up being a convenient proxy for it, especially in the absence of other clear indicators. However, it is a poor proxy, and we ignore the true, objective indicators of leadership talent and performance at our peril.

As we might expect, research shows that—like attractiveness—the importance of charisma as a leadership signal decreases when followers have more information on the leaders. For example, voters are often surprised—sometimes even upset—when they complete surveys designed to match their personal values and beliefs to the political candidate that best represents them. If the voters want someone aligned with their economic, social, and political views, the appropriate candidate is often not the one they felt emotionally drawn to. Conversely, when we judge leaders purely on the basis of their TV appearances and Twitter feeds, charisma rules, overshadowing any logical arguments.

Another example of the irrational power of charisma, academic studies show that charismatic CEOs can inflate their companies' stock price, even when, by objective indicators, their companies are not performing well.[20] Henry Tosi at the University of Florida and colleagues asked managers from fifty-nine US firms how charismatic their CEOs were, using a well-validated peer-report measure of charisma. They also looked at their firms' performance, such as shareholder value and return on assets. Although charisma ratings were unrelated to firm performance, they were pos-itively linked to firm size . . . and CEO compensation! And despite a positive correlation between charisma ratings and stock valuation during uncertain market conditions, there was no association between charisma and actual firm per-formance (irrespective of the market conditions).

CHAPTER **5**

The Female Advantage

Thus far, we've reviewed the research indicating that men are more likely to be overconfident, narcissists, and psychopathic than women. Even when such differences are small, they are still reliable and meaningful, particularly in shaping collective leadership preferences.

We've also seen that all these traits, while they help you achieve a leadership role, hurt your performance once you are in that role. And we've explored the slippery nature of charisma and seen how rather than being an inborn trait that some leaders just have (or don't have), it's something that followers tend to project onto their leaders, in particular when they are male.

If confidence is not competence, charisma is a mirage, and traits like narcissism and psychopathy hurt more than help leaders' performance and especially their followers, it is only natural to wonder: could women just be better suited to leadership roles?

Some people think so. In an interview at the World Economic Forum in Davos, Jack Ma, the iconic founder of Alibaba, was asked what he thought of the shortage of women in leadership.[1] He said that he didn't understand why companies, including technology firms, did not employ more women. Mr. Ma noted that at Alibaba, 49 percent of staff and almost 37 percent of senior leaders are female, which is possibly a record for a big high-tech firm. Ma then spelled out his theory of leadership: "Men have high IQ but low EQ [emotional intelligence]," whereas women "are balanced across both." Leaving aside the backhanded compliment to women's IQs, Ma's comment underscores the stereotype of women as more emotional and men as more cerebral. It's also congruent with the now widely held view that EQ is a central quality for effective leadership.

In this chapter, we explore these interrelated ideas. What are the competence differences, if any, between men and women, and how might they influence potential gender differences in leadership performance? Do women on average truly have higher EQs? And does a higher EQ benefit leaders, both male and female? Finally, we'll take a closer look at some specific leadership behaviors enabled by EQ: transformational leadership, personal effectiveness, and self-awareness.

Why men and women are both from Earth

In *Men Are from Mars, Women Are from Venus,* one of the best-selling self-help books of all time, John Gray postulated that men and women are so profoundly different that they may as well come from different planets—yes, the clue is in the title. For example, he writes, women are overly sensitive and caring, whereas men are not in touch with their inner emotional lives and are fixated on competition. While these stereotypical gender differences are largely consistent with the research on overconfidence, narcissism, and psychopathy highlighted in previous chapters, there are more psychological similarities than differences between men and women. This point is important. Even when a statistical difference implies that groups are not equal, that still leaves plenty of room for similarities between individuals from both groups. To use a different example, women tend to live longer than men, but most men and women die at a similar age. By the same token, men are generally taller than women, but many women in the world are taller than most men.

In 2005, Janet Shelby Hyde, a prolific psychologist at the University of Wisconsin–Madison known for her pioneering research on large data sets on gender differences, reanalyzed forty-six meta-analyses on gender differences in competence. Crunching the data from millions of participants, she examined every domain of competence and ability ever studied. In an age where the proliferation of independent studies has led to concerns about the "replication crisis" in the social sciences, as the vast volume of research enables people to cherry-pick their findings and indulge in selective reporting, this review is *the* go-to resource for anyone interested in accessing the most reliable evidence on how men and women differ.[2]

Its main findings? In 78 percent of the cases, gender differences are either null or very small.[3] The fact that these studies were conducted in areas where gender differences were historically assumed and that the studies include data from many decades ago makes the reported similarities all the more remarkable. And the findings apply to a wide range of psychological variables, including attitudes, motivation, personality, and job performance.

A focal point of Hyde's study concerned gender differences in IQ. Here, too, results revealed negligible differences between the sexes, though men have a clear advantage of women in spatial ability tests; this difference is largely caused by testosterone differences between men and women.[4] Indeed, women with higher testosterone levels outperform men with lower testosterone levels on spatial intelligence measures, and injecting either men or women with testosterone improves their performance on spatial ability and map-reading ability tests. On the other hand, women score higher on most verbal ability tests. But generally speaking, there are no salient IQ differences between men and women.

Intellectually, then, women and men have no differences in capacity. But how do they compare in other areas of life, such as physical, emotional, or social skills?

Hyde's definitive study did find that in 22 percent of cases, women and men differed: men can throw an object further and faster than women can; men tend to masturbate more frequently (or at least they are more inclined to report it); and men tend to have a more positive view of casual sex. Men were also more physically aggressive, although the data on relational aggression—think *Mean Girls*—was more mixed.

But unless you work in a very unusual industry, a leadership position at your organization probably does not require a leader to be especially good at throwing things, having casual sex, or self-pleasure. So, let's leave those topics behind and take a closer look at any gender differences in leadership-oriented qualities.

For instance, women have slightly higher leadership potential in that they generally perform better in management and leadership roles than men do, even when men see themselves as better leaders than women.[5] These differences in leadership competence are also consistent with gender differences in vocational interests, particularly women's preferences for working with people and men's preferences for working with things. These divergent preferences represent one of the biggest psychological gender differences ever reported.[6]

Women's better performance in leadership roles alone should suggest something odd about the gender imbalance in leadership, which is all about working with people rather than things. But illogically, this point is often emphasized by diversity skeptics seeking to undermine organizational efforts to correct the underrepresentation of women in leadership. For example, in the infamous memo that got engineer James Damore fired from Google, in which he strenuously objected to the organization's diversity program, he correctly observed that psychological studies indicate that "women on average show a higher interest in people and men in things."[7]

What about the stereotype that women are more caring than men and have higher interpersonal or emotional skills? Although gender differences in EQ are far from substantial, with average differences rarely exceeding 15 percent, they do overwhelmingly favor women.

How EQ helps (women) at work

In 1990, Yale social psychologist Peter Salovey and University of New Hampshire psychology professor John D. Mayer coined the term *emotional intelligence*. Five years later, science journalist Daniel Goleman popularized the concept with his best-selling book. Emotional intelligence, or EQ, concerns the ability to understand and manage your own and other people's emotions; it is the best single measure of people skills. Despite attracting little academic research during its first decade, EQ rapidly became the darling of HR and leadership competencies. There is now a vast body of research on EQ: over forty-three hundred scientific studies have been published since the early 2000s, compared with just ninety in the 1990s.

A substantial proportion of these studies examined the performance implications of EQ. For example, consistent evidence suggests that EQ plays a central role in individuals' employability, that is, their ability to gain and maintain a job.[8] Since work (still) involves interacting with people, and given that people's career success is primarily determined by what other people think of them, individuals who are more rewarding to deal with can be expected to do better across a wide range of jobs, particularly those with a strong interpersonal component, for example, sales, public relations, customer service, management, and leadership.

EQ has also been positively linked to a wide range of outcomes related to employee well-being. For example, people with higher EQ are more likely to be engaged at work.[9] Given the prevalence of employee disengagement and the growing problem of employee stress and burnout (a case of extreme disengagement), an engaged workforce is no small feat. If organizations wanted to boost employee engagement, there is probably no better way than to hire people with high EQ. Such a hiring strategy would not necessarily translate into higher performance, but it would mean a more satisfied or patient workforce!

EQ also strongly predicts people's resilience and tolerance to stress. In fact, a higher EQ is a good antidote to the dark side of personality and the toxic behaviors described earlier. EQ is represents the flip side of both narcissism and psychopathy, and individuals with a higher EQ are also less likely to be overconfident, excitable, moody, and irritable at work. These calmer aspects of people's personalities are particularly helpful in management. How can you manage others when you have difficulties managing yourself? EQ helps solve both problems.

It's commonly assumed that IQ and EQ don't go together, that people with high IQs will be socially awkward and that people with high EQs aren't very smart. Little scientific evidence supports this idea, as EQ and IQ are *not* negatively related. Of course, some academically smart people—particularly those with high IQs—may no doubt come across as somewhat odd or at least eccentric to the average person. Simon Baron-Cohen, at the University of Cambridge, compellingly demonstrated that people with very high IQs often have interpersonal deficits.[10] But we might also remember these high-IQ/low-EQ cases precisely because they stand out; they are the exceptions that confirm the rule.

As we would expect, individuals with higher EQs are generally more effective in leadership roles. Studies have found a consistent positive association between EQ and organizational citizenship behaviors, so the probability that leaders will behave well and engage in prosocial behaviors while refraining from toxic activities increases with their EQ. While EQ is not a perfect predictor of integrity, if an organization hired leaders on the basis of their high EQs, it would end up with leaders who were more honest and ethical.

Despite the small gender differences for EQ, as a group, women do tend to have higher EQs than men do. The effect has been reliably found across virtually all measures of EQ. In fact, a recent meta-analysis of gender differences in EQ went as far as to conclude that selecting employees and leaders according to EQ would severely hurt men. But we can hardly call a focus on EQ reverse discrimination. Other things being equal, higher-EQ individuals deserve to be promoted, whether they are male or female.[11]

In addition, three important leadership competencies that are enabled by higher EQs have been found at higher rates in women: transformational leadership, personal effectiveness, and self-awareness. We'll now take a closer look at each of these competencies.

Transformational leadership

Both male leaders with higher EQs and most women leaders display a more transformational leadership style. With this style, the leader focuses on changing followers' attitudes and beliefs and engaging them on a deep emotional level rather than telling them what to do—think Michelle Obama or Oprah Winfrey. Leaders better able to identify and manage emotions are also better able to motivate others, and most of the variability in transformational leadership arises from levels of EQ.[12]

Transformational leaders excel at turning a vision into an actionable plan for change, and they are strong role models for their subordinates and followers. Moreover, leaders and other people with higher EQs are also better at the transactional elements of leadership such as assigning tasks, monitoring and managing employees' performance, and setting rewards and incentives.

On the other hand, both leaders with lower EQs and male leaders are more likely to take a laissez-faire approach. This style of leadership, characterized by an absent leader, usually impairs a team's morale and performance, leaving employees without a sense of direction and purpose. In summary, positive leadership styles are associated with high-EQ leaders and most female leaders, whereas negative leadership styles are associated with low-EQ leaders and most male leaders.

A recent study showed that gender affects leadership outcomes and effectiveness because of the gender differences in EQ. Largely because women have higher EQs, women's teams are more engaged and outperform those led by men.[13] Perhaps more surprisingly, even leadership styles purportedly associated with men, such as entrepreneurial or disruptive approaches, are more likely to emerge in higher-EQ leaders.

Of course, all these indicators of superior female performance could partly be caused by the tougher selection criteria operating on women than on men. If tougher criteria are truly being applied to women, then there are few better arguments for implementing similar selection standards on male leaders.

Personal effectiveness

Although EQ was originally considered a form of intelligence, strong evidence suggests that it mostly represents individuals' *personal effectiveness*, or the ability to navigate everyday interpersonal challenges successfully, both emotionally and socially. Clearly, personal effectiveness requires a minimum degree of self-control and resilience, critical elements of EQ. In addition, EQ is strongly associated with empathy, the ability to know what other people are feeling and thinking. And to be effective in any aspect of your personal life, you need to be able to influence others; empathy helps you do so.

Female leaders have more empathy than male leaders do. Regardless of the type of empathy evaluated, most women, from a young age, have more empathy than men have; this difference between genders is larger than for most other personality traits.[14] Empathic leaders' ability to see problems from other people's perspectives makes them less self-centered and more flexible in problem solving.

You can think of life as a real IQ test. But in real life, the problems you face are not well defined, nor do they have a definitive correct answer. For instance, should you tell your boss that you want a pay increase? How can you motivate an employee who seems a bit down? And what is the best way to engage an audience during a presentation?

As much as we would like to find logical and seemingly objective answers to these and other real-life challenges, and despite the thousands of self-help books and YouTube videos pretending to know the answers, we cannot know in advance the correct responses to all life's quandaries. And even after we judge the outcome of certain actions, we can never be sure what results the alternative decisions would have produced.

These constraints make personality the best source of data to predict individuals' likelihood to handle themselves more effectively across different situations. So, even if we don't know what the best answers to these questions are, certain people seem to find those answers more often than others, and the most generalizable quality they have is higher EQ.

For example, the resilience typical in leaders with EQ helps them cope with the high pressure they experience and bounce back from adversity. As Sheryl Sandberg discloses in her recent book, *Option B: Facing Adversity, Building Resilience, and Finding Joy* (coauthored with Adam Grant), the Facebook chief operating officer had to recover from the loss of her husband, who died suddenly from a heart problem while they were on vacation.[15] What is the best thing to do when we face such tragic and devastating events? Unlike IQ tests, life has no predefined correct answers. And even if there were, what are the chances that someone could actually put these answers into practice in the throes of life's challenges?

Instead, bouncing back from difficult moments is an EQ problem. The challenge is about remaining composed and finding a way to maintain personal effectiveness during horrible and destabilizing circumstances. Even for Sandberg, the answer was far from clear. But her resilience and higher EQ enabled her to keep her composure and try out options until she found one that worked. In the end, she shared her story and feelings with others, first in a blog and then with her book.[16] The implication here is not that others in similar situations should follow suit, but that any leader will be more likely to find a solution that works if he or she has a high EQ. For the same reasons, we would expect Sandberg to bounce back from future adversities in the spirit of her nickname, "the Teflon leader."

A big part of personal effectiveness, including resilience, is self-control, and decades of psychological research show that from an early age, women display higher levels of self-control than men do, not least because girls and women have less license to be themselves than men do.[17] In leaders, self-control is an important antidote to abuses of power and other toxic behaviors. In fact, most antisocial behaviors are partly indicative of people's inability to contain their short-term impulses—instant gratification—in favor of less problematic and more beneficial long-term goals.

For an interesting historical lesson on the benefits of self-control, consider the 2008 global financial melt-down, which led to the collapse of major financial institutions, the loss of millions of jobs and homes, and the biggest government bailout in history. These effects were particularly noticeable in Iceland, a country with a tiny population that had enjoyed meteoric economic growth in the decade before the crisis, when its banking system had grown from 100 percent to 900 percent of GDP. Two female bankers who were appalled by the risk-taking of their male colleagues decided to launch Audur Capital, a financial services firm that aimed to promote "feminine" values in banking. Congruent with this mission, Audur took a much more cautious approach to investing, keeping away from distressed debt and toxic junk bonds. As a result, it was the only Icelandic company that emerged unscathed from the crisis. And although Iceland was already a leading nation on gender equality, the success of Audur played a big role in further increasing the representation of women—including leaders—at work: from 2008 to 2017, Iceland has topped the World Economic Forum's gender equality index, and two of Iceland's recent prime ministers have been women (compared with none before the crisis).

Consistent with Iceland's experience, a study published in 2009 by CERAM, a French business school, showed that the presence of women leaders in banking tends to have a positive effect on their firms, limiting the risky behaviors and greedy excesses of men. To be more precise, banks with a higher ratio of women in top management were more resilient to the financial crisis. This benefit was also reflected in a smaller drop in share price in the aftermath of the crisis. For instance, French international banking group BNP Paribas, where 39 percent of managers were women, saw its stock fall by 20 percent, whereas Crédit Agricole, where only 16 percent of managers are women, saw it plummet by 50 percent.[18]

A related aspect of personal effectiveness enhanced by EQ concerns anger management. While we often think that there are quick and effective methods to tame someone's anger or aggression, these intense negative emotions are mostly a function of an individual's personality. Of course, we all get angry or aggressive under certain circumstances, but two individuals in the same situation will react differently, and this difference depends on their EQ. The higher EQ in most women explains why they are less volatile than men. Extensive research has linked gender differences in aggressiveness to testosterone, which is systematically higher in men than women.[19] In fact, merely exposing men to women inhibits their testosterone bursts, making men less aggressive and helping them delay gratification.

Self-awareness

Self-awareness has historically been defined as introspection or the process of looking inside yourself to enhance your self-knowledge. While this aspect of self-awareness is no doubt useful, a more consequential side concerns understanding how you affect others and, in turn, what others think of you. As the poet Maya Angelou noted, "When someone shows you who they are, believe them." In that sense, self-awareness is really about *other*-awareness, and people with higher EQs are better able to understand how their actions affect and are perceived by others. Such understanding provides the foundations for any development and coaching interventions. If you really want to understand yourself, skip the six months in an ashram in India, and instead pay attention to how other people see you.

Just like with health and happiness, the importance of self-awareness is most evident when it is missing. Think of the David Brent or Michael Scott characters from the fictional but hyper-realistic series *The Office*; the humor in both the British and the American versions of this sitcom entirely relies on these characters' cluelessness about how they come across. In contrast, because self-aware leaders understand what others make of them, these leaders can pick a more effective range of behaviors and successfully manage their reputations.

To measure leaders' self-awareness, we can calculate the difference between their self-views and other people's views of them. Any well-designed 360-degree analysis can assess this difference. A literature review suggests that this gap is larger in male leaders than in female leaders, with men's self-ratings around 0.3 of a standard deviation higher than women's. This statistic means that 62 percent of men can be expected to rate themselves higher than the average woman.[20] Remarkably, both more accurate and more *critical* self-views—rating yourself more negatively than others rate you—are associated with superior leadership performance. A leader who underrates his or her own performance is more likely to be a better leader, perhaps because the individual's humility and relative insecurity will motivate him or her to work harder to succeed.

As with so many other differences between men and women, women's higher self-awareness—and greater likelihood of seeing themselves in a worse light than others see them—is usually lamented as just one more thing that ambitious women will have to fix or get over. Women do report higher levels of depression and anxiety, and people can worry too much about what others think of them. And yes, it's a challenge for many female leaders to learn to cope with the greater scrutiny and judgment they face. But the upshot of living under a microscope—and learning to see yourself as others see you—may be that it helps women become better leaders.

CHAPTER 6

What Good Leaders Look Like

If you were a barista in the cafés of Edinburgh in the 1990s, you might have gotten to know a thirty-something single mom named Joanne. She would come into your café, order a cup of coffee, and then sit for a couple of hours and write, sometimes bringing her sleeping baby daughter with her. Perhaps you would ask how the writing was going, and she would tell you that yet another publisher had turned her down.

Talent is notoriously hard to spot. If it weren't, twelve publishers would not have passed on Joanne's books, which have now sold more than four hundred million copies worldwide. Perhaps you know her better as J. K. Rowling, creator of the Harry Potter series.

There is no questioning her talents; seven out of the top twenty best-selling books of all time are hers, and these books account for combined sales of over five hundred million copies, far more than any other author.[1] And yet, Rowling only managed to publish her first book at the age of thirty-seven, in exchange for a $2,000 advance, after being rejected by so many publishers that clearly failed to see her potential.

Before we get too far, let's distinguish potential from talent. Regardless of the domain of competence—sports, military, science, arts, or business—talent generally denotes superior performance in a given field. When individuals accomplish extraordinary things in their profession and when these accomplishments cannot be fully attributed to other factors, such as work, luck, or nepotism, we refer to these people as talented. Potential, on the other hand, is talent in waiting, or nascent talent. It is talent before you can see it, talent before it happens. Organizations would be wise to see potential as more valuable than talent, because they are in fierce competition to identify future leaders as early as possible, and before their competitors do.

Of particular importance here is the question of whether an individual who has not yet led can be a good leader. In this context, potential is really a bet that organizations place on an individual's ability to display leadership talent in the future—and they cannot rely on past performance to predict this potential when individuals have not done the job yet.

Most organizations rely on oversimplified models of leadership potential, focusing too much on a single factor—usually the latest HR fad—while ignoring the wider range of determinants of leadership. Amazon reportedly optimizes for curiosity, Twitter and Silicon Valley obsess over growth mindset, American Express wants to hire on grit, and the list of organizations that equate leadership potential with learning agility is too long to mention. More and more organizations are developing their own indicators of potential, usually under the label of "competency frameworks." The indicators are a hybrid between genuine talent-identification philosophies and elaborate PR manifestos that often represent wishful thinking.

Conversely, scientific theories of leadership often develop in isolation from real-world business problems and with little regard for practical implementation. This gap between science and practice is, of course, nothing new. As philosopher of science Karl Popper once noted, models can be accurate or useful, but rarely both.

What do we really know, then, about the essence of leadership potential? Despite vast and scattered research on leadership, much evidence suggests some common attributes that effective leaders have. We can distill these qualities into essential categories or "buckets" of leadership potential to predict an individual's likelihood of becoming an effective leader. Within the literature, the best kind of studies are meta-analyses, which aggregate the results from hundreds—if not thousands—of independent studies comparing the attributes that best differentiate effective and ineffective leaders. Drawing from these studies, I present three evidence-based generalizations that should help organizations pick better leaders.

Intellectual capital

Good leadership requires *intellectual capital*. The key components of intellectual capital—domain-specific expertise, experience, and good judgment—not only enable leaders to perform their specific roles, but also give them credibility with their followers. The German philosopher Martin Heidegger once noted that the main difference between individuals with and without expertise is that the former can quickly ignore the irrelevant aspects of a problem. Imagine an expert looking at a chess board, a wine shop, or the cockpit of a Boeing 747. Unlike a novice, a person with strong intellectual capital will quickly focus on the relevant components of a situation, while a novice would get distracted by irrelevant features, mistaking noise for signals. Individuals with strong intellectual capital are also more able to rely on their instincts when they have to solve work-related problems because experience and expertise have made their intuition more data-driven. But, by definition, experts are a minority.

As a series of studies led by Amanda Goodall from City, University of London, showed, organizations do better when led by experts in the field. Hospitals have better outcomes if their leaders are doctors rather than businesspeople or finance people. In sports, basketball teams perform better when managed by an all-star basketball player, and Formula One teams win more if they are managed by successful former racing drivers.[2] Similarly, universities are more likely to excel when their presidents have a background in science and research rather than being career administrators.[3]

Leaders' intellectual capital affects team performance by boosting team morale and employee engagement. For instance, a recent study led by Benjamin Artz from the University of Wisconsin examined the connection between leaders' technical expertise and the well-being of their teams. Artz and colleagues looked at thirty-five thousand employees from a wide range of US and UK organizations. To evaluate the technical expertise of leaders, they asked employees to rate statements such as "If needed, my boss would be able to do my job pretty well" and "My boss worked his/her way up in the company." Their analyses revealed that leaders' technical expertise was the single most important predictor of their subordinates' engagement—even more than their salary! Moreover, by examining longitudinal data from teams that changed leaders, Artz and his team highlighted a clear causal effect: when a newly appointed leader inherited an established team in the organization, the morale of the team rose if the new leader had higher levels of technical expertise than his or her predecessor had.[4]

The good news is that organizations are generally aware of the importance of intellectual capital. As we would expect, meta-analytic reviews confirm that formal qualifications and credentials predict whether someone emerges as leader. The reviews also show that at all levels of seniority, individuals' technical competence and experience predict not only their future job performance, but also higher levels of creativity, prosocial behaviors within the organization, and fewer counterproductive work behaviors. More-qualified leaders are also paid more, get promoted and chosen for coaching and training programs more often, and switch jobs more often, not least because they have more choices than their less qualified counterparts.[5]

The bad news is that for all the talk of the importance of EQ and "soft skills," organizations tend to over-rely on technical expertise. Not that technical expertise doesn't matter. Clearly, as we've just discussed, it does. But it is not sufficient for identifying leadership potential, particularly when employees make the transition from individual contributors to managers or leaders. Whether it is in Wall Street, pharma, or Silicon Valley, every technical industry with high-complexity jobs that require high IQs suffers from the same problem: a surplus of technical experts with limited leadership talent. Past performance is usually a good predictor of future performance, except when the context changes. And, *quelle surprise*, when you move people from a role that requires working independently and solving well-defined, algorithmic problems to a role that requires leading others, most people will stop performing as well as they did before.

Another reason not to rely too heavily on intelligence is that as machine learning and artificial intelligence (AI) grow more sophisticated, they'll be able to solve intellectual puzzles better than we can. Paradoxically, the AI age will probably end up emphasizing the emotional side of leadership: since leaders cannot outperform machines in managing data, information, or well-defined problems, they will predominantly compete in terms of their ability to manage people.

Social capital

Even when leaders show strong potential regarding their intellectual capital, their *social capital* is key. Social capital concerns the network and connections that leaders have at their disposal. As David Ogilvy, the wizard advertising tycoon who inspired the *Mad Men* character of Don Draper used to say, "Contacts mean contracts." Who you know determines not just how you lead, but also whether you lead at all, wherever you operate.

Much research in organizational psychology suggests that individuals are more effective as leaders when they have wider and deeper connections within and outside their organizations.[6] Since leadership is, at its core, a process of influence, those who form broader and richer relationships with others will undoubtedly be in a better position to influence. In fact, research suggests that one of the best single indicators of a leader's influence—not just in business but also in politics and the military—is how central the person is in the organization's network.[7] You can calculate people's network centrality using traditional self-report questionnaires. You ask the members of the organization how close they are to others, where they go for advice, and who they regard as a source of knowledge and expertise. Alternatively, you can use passive measures, such as contextual email data: how many people you regularly connect with, how often, and how interconnected they are.

Consider an individual whose habitual email traffic shows that he or she is connects with a larger and more diverse group of people who are themselves not strongly interconnected through their own habitual email exchanges. We could expect this person to exert more influence and have more leadership potential than someone who is only connected with a small group of interconnected people. Thus the success and influence of leaders tend to increase with the depth and density of their network. As the saying (often attributed to Johann Wolfgang von Goethe) goes, "a great person attracts great people and knows how to hold them together."

The importance of social capital is also reflected in the value that most people still assign to personal referrals and letters of recommendation. The opinions of others still carry great weight in leader selection. Although meta-analyses suggest that references are not a strong predictor of job performance, any candidate for a position will struggle to compete against a person who comes strongly recommended or endorsed by someone close to the decision maker.[8] People trust word of mouth in any area of life, and leadership potential is no exception. And even though most people are not very good at judging this potential, their opinion has consequences.

Decisions based on a person's social capital may be subtle and implicit, such as when hiring managers praise a candidate for a "strong culture fit." They really mean that the person appears to be part of whatever tribe or in-group the hiring manager—and dominant group—belongs to. Unspoken indicators for such strong culture fit may include a person's school affiliation (e.g., an Ivy League institution strongly represented in the organization); technical background (e.g., engineering, law, an MBA); or religious affiliation or ethnicity. Perhaps even more importantly, social capital is usually confounded with a person's socioeconomic status not just in countries that have historically been quite explicit about this—India and Britain—but also in those that embrace strong meritocratic ideals. For example, in the United States, 50 percent of a person's career success is determined by his or her parents' career success. As recently noted by Matthew Stewart in the *Atlantic*: "In America, the game is half over once you've selected your parents."[9] The tight link between success and socioeconomic level, of course, has not always been the case. Until the 1970s, thirty-year-old Americans had a 90 percent chance of earning more than their parents earned, which is as close to certain upward mobility as you can get. That figure is now only 50 percent.[10]

Psychological capital

Finally, good leadership requires *psychological capital*, that is, how individuals will lead and whether they will make use of their capabilities. To answer these questions, we need to understand leaders on three core dimensions of character: the bright side, the dark side, and the inside of a person's personality.[11]

The bright side

The *bright side* comprises intelligence, which is a person's general learning ability, and the major personality traits, such as extraversion and ambition, that account for individuals' typical predispositions. This side reflects what people do when they are at their best, and what they usually do at work when they are making an effort to display their best character attributes.

According to meta-analyses of fifty years of research on the key psychological capital predictors of leadership effectiveness, bright side personality traits such as curiosity, extraversion, and emotional stability explain around 40 percent of the variability between leaders' performance.[12] A separate meta-analysis showed that intelligence—which is unrelated to personality—also predicts individual differences in leadership.[13] These findings do not imply that leaders must have all these traits to have potential, but those who do have these traits are much more likely to be effective.

Even a few defining bright side traits can make a big impact in shaping leaders' footprints. Consider, for example, Nelson Mandela's emotional stability, which explains how he could serve twenty-seven unjust years in prison and forgive his enemies when he was released. Or Coco

Chanel's ambition, which enabled her to escape from poverty to create one of the most admired luxury brands in history. Or Jeff Bezos's curiosity, which has made Amazon one of the most innovative companies in the world, and Bezos the richest man in history.

The dark side

The *dark side* captures less desirable aspects of personality, such as the already-examined traits of narcissism and psychopathy, that hinder a leader's ability to build and maintain a high-performing team and contribute to the long-term success of the team and organization. Consider that in any industry at any given point, there is no shortage of leaders who are technically brilliant, well networked, who clearly have a super successful bright side, but who are nonetheless unable to control the counterproductive or self-destructive elements of their personality. As mentioned in chapter 3, narcissism and psychopathy are two dark side traits commonly associated with leadership, but there are many others, too.

In 1997, psychologists Robert and Joyce Hogan created a scientifically defensible methodology for evaluating narcissism, psychopathy, and nine other dark side traits that cause leaders to derail. Since then their related assessment, the Hogan Development Survey, licensed by the eponymous company Hogan Assessments, has been widely adopted to pinpoint leaders' coaching and development needs.[14]

After profiling millions of people, Hogan's data suggests that most individuals display at least three of these dark side traits. What's more, about 40 percent score high enough on one or two traits to put them at risk for future career derailment—even if they're currently successful and effective.

Dark side traits can be divided into three groups. The first group is the *distancing traits*—obvious turn-offs that push leaders away from other people. Being highly excitable and moody has this effect, for instance; or having a deeply skeptical, cynical outlook, which makes it hard to build trust. Another example is leisurely passive-aggressiveness—pretending to have a relaxed, polite attitude while actually resisting cooperation or even engaging in backstabbing.

The second group of traits has, in contrast, *seductive qualities*; they are geared to draw people in. These traits are often found in assertive, charismatic leaders, who gather followers or gain influence with bosses through their ability to manage up. Narcissism and psychopathy are in this group.

The third group contains *ingratiating traits*, which can have a positive connotation in followers but rarely do in leaders. Someone who is diligent, for instance, may try to impress the boss with meticulous attention to detail, but this attention can also translate into preoccupation with petty matters or micromanagement of the person's own direct reports. Someone who is dutiful and eager to please those in authority can easily become too submissive.

The inside

The *inside* of leaders' personality concerns their values, which function as an internal moral compass and determine how well the leaders will fit in with the culture of the organization and what type of culture they will create. For example, leaders who value tradition will have a strong sense of right and wrong, will prefer hierarchical organizations, and will have little tolerance of disruption and innovation. Put them in a creative environment, and they will struggle. On the other hand, leaders who value affiliation will have a strong desire to get along with others and will focus on building and maintaining strong interpersonal relationships and on working collaboratively. These leaders will not be engaged if their roles are too isolated and the company cultures are overly individualistic. Finally, altruistic leaders will strive to improve other people's lives and drive progress in the world, so they will suffer if their organizations are purely driven by profits.

Summing up, if someone has the right intellectual capital, social capital, and psychological capital, they will have more potential to be a good leader. But it's not guaranteed. Here's why.

Leadership talent: personality in the right place

Even if the essence of leadership talent is universal, the context a leader is in will shape how they behave, ought to behave, and are evaluated.

As a consequence, some leaders may be popular in some cultures but not in others (think Vladimir Putin or Hugo Chávez), and many high-performing managers may struggle when they are moved from one culture to another, for example, from Germany to Indonesia or from a nongovernmental organization to a fintech startup.

To use a couple of famous examples, Winston Churchill was a brilliant leader during wartime, when his stubbornness and paranoia were valuable traits, but he was far less effective during peaceful times—for the same reasons. Walt Disney was fired from his journalist position with the *Kansas City Star* newspaper for lacking any good ideas, according to his boss. Oprah Winfrey was fired from her first TV anchor job for being "too emotionally invested" in her stories. And in July 2018, Donald Trump enjoyed a mere 8 percent approval rating among Democrats but an 87 percent rating among Republicans. It is hard to find a better current example of a polarizing leader, and polarization implies that performance—or at least our views of it—is contextual. If talent is personality in the right place, then the context obviously matters as much as the leader's personality does.

For this reason, researchers examine the relationship between leadership and culture. This relationship is defined loosely as the standards about how people should behave and what they should value and approve of in a given setting. Organizations now commonly advertise their cultural tenets in the form of public manifestos: Google's "Don't be evil," Facebook's "Move fast and break things," Apple's

"Think different," and older ones such as GE's "Stay lean to go fast," Toyota's "Kaizen," and IKEA's "Humbleness and willpower."

These statements reflect organizations' attempt to translate their cultures into simple mantras that provide a higher-order code of conduct to guide employees' behaviors and reduce uncertainty. One of the simplest and best descriptions of culture is Google's "how we do things around here." An organization's culture reflects its leaders' values, particularly its founders' values.[15] In fact, all the above taglines apply as much to the cultures of those organizations as they do to the philosophies of their founders. For example, when US senators asked Mark Zuckerberg to explain a privacy breach in Facebook data, the CEO and founder justified it by saying that any company that grows so fast will inevitably make mistakes—in other words, "break things." Thus, there is as much variability in groups' and organizations' cultures as there is in individuals' values.

So, how does leadership vary across cultures? Although all cultures including small and medium-sized businesses, *Fortune* 100 companies, and nations—are better served by leaders with more rather than less integrity, competence, and people skills, at a more granular level, some differences in leadership style will also make someone more effective as a leader. The classic framework to understand these stylistic differences is social psychologist Geert Hofstede's culture model, which he developed through a comparison of the different attitudes and values of IBM people around the world.[16] This model identified four major aspects of cultural differences in work-related behaviors, including leadership:

> DOMINANCE: Cultures differ in their degree of domi-
> nance, with dominant cultures embracing assertive,
> overconfident, and authoritarian leaders. As we
> would expect, this dimension of culture is asso-
> ciated with stronger preferences for male leaders
> and greater resistance to female leaders. Moreover,
> high-dominance cultures will be less receptive to
> male leaders who behave in more consultative,
> nurturing, empathic ways, with clear implications
> for gender diversity: dominant cultures will have
> no problem being led only by men and expecting
> those men to behave in stereotypically masculine
> ways. Examples of high-dominance national cultures
> include Mexico, Japan, and Nigeria; low-dominance
> nations include Sweden, Iceland, and Norway.[17]
> Industry sectors characterized by high-dominance
> cultures include banking, law, and the military,
> whereas low-dominance industries include educa-
> tion, public relations, and nonprofits.

> SPONTANEITY: Cultures also differ in their level
> of comfort with spontaneity and improvisation.
> Spontaneous cultures embrace uncertainty. They
> don't need to plan everything, and they can function
> without a clear set of rules or well-defined processes.
> To succeed in these cultures, leaders will need to be

highly adaptable and skilled improvisers. In contrast, cultures lacking spontaneity will be rule bound and will impose a clear set of rules on both employees and leaders, who will tend to experience uncertainty and discomfort when required to make independent decisions. Examples of spontaneous national cultures include Argentina and Brazil; nations with more-cautious cultures include Singapore and Japan. In general, high-spontaneity cultures will favor male leaders, as men are less conscientious, organized, and risk-averse than women.

INDIVIDUALISM: As the everyday meaning of the word denotes, individualistic cultures reward independent actions and tend to celebrate the achievements of individuals rather than teams. In such cultures, the boundaries between in-groups and out-groups will be relatively loose, and leaders will be praised for their nonconformity and originality. Standing out, a desirable goal for both employees and leaders, is generally a disadvantage for group activity. As we would expect, people aspire to leadership more often in individualistic cultures, because leadership in itself is regarded as a way of standing out from the crowd. Conversely, collectivistic cultures focus on team rather than individual accomplishments and have stronger preferences for leaders who are low-key and humble. Leaders in individualistic cultures will be given more leeway to make single-handed decisions and have procedural power, while collectivistic cultures will relish consensual and democratic decision making. Examples of individualistic countries include the United States, the United Kingdom, and Australia; collectivistic countries include China, South Korea, and Indonesia. Individualism is a prominent cultural tenet in banking and academia, whereas collectivism is more common in the military and professional sports. In general, individualistic cultures will benefit male leaders, as women are generally more team oriented and collectivistic, both as employees and as leaders.

STATUS: Cultures also differ in their acceptance of status. In particular, status-oriented cultures regard big power differences between individuals as natural and accept that certain people will always be better off than others. When leaders emerge in such cultures, they will be given more privileges and authority. In such cultures, social and economic inequalities will be greater and subordinates will be more likely to accept a leader on the basis of his or her social status, rather than talents. By the same token, subordinates in such cultures generally hesitate to criticize their leaders, so the leaders will rarely benefit from upward feedback or constructive criticism from those who report to them. In contrast, cultures with low status orientation will be more egalitarian and meritocratic. They will be more willing to accept gender diversity and tolerate—perhaps even choose—leaders from outside the status quo. Examples of status-accepting national cultures include China, India, and Nigeria; countries that reject natural status differences include the Netherlands, Germany, and Denmark. High-status sectors include the military, civil services, and health care, and low-status industries include media, including entertainment, and the tech startup world. Because high-status cultures tend to embrace tradition and the status quo, it will be generally harder for women to emerge as leaders in such cultures.

Ultimately, if organizations want to crack the formula for effective leadership at the most detailed level, they can safely ignore the broader categories of culture, such as country, sector, and even company practices, and benchmark high-performing leaders within desired roles. Assuming an organization has enough examples of, and past data on, high- and low-performing leaders, it can uncover what makes a good (and bad) leader in a given role. Of course, what has worked in the past may not necessarily work in the future. But organizations tend to magnify the impact of change and obsess over changing circumstances. This attitude often distracts groups from getting the basics right or becomes an excuse for not even trying.

Getting the basics right

If the formula for leadership potential is not that complex and the essence of leadership talent is almost universal, why can't more organizations get it right? To get it right and improve the quality of their leaders, organizations must address five common mistakes in how they view leadership (table 6-1). As the table shows, organizations often define a leader as the person in charge or in a formal position of power. But the evidence-based view of a leader is that of someone able to align a group in the pursuit of a common goal. Accordingly, some people may not be in a position of authority but may act as leaders by encouraging people to work together as a coordinated unit. Likewise, some individuals formally in charge may not be operating as leaders or may have little talent for shaping a winning team. This conflict between true ability and a leadership assignment often arises when employees are rewarded with a leadership role because of their past performance as individual contributors. Under these circumstances, leadership is more of a symbolic title or recognition for past efforts, rather than an actual resource for the team or organization.

As noted in the table, the key goal of a good leader is not to get to the top of a group or an organization, but to help the team outperform its rivals. While this goal is obvious for professional sports, which have a clear set of rules and objectives and whose performance you can judge with objectivity, this goal is not so obvious in most organizations.

TABLE 6-1

Leadership: common (and mistaken) perception versus the scientific view of leadership

Aspect of leadership	Common perception	Evidence-based view
Definition of leader	Person in charge or with power	Person who builds a winning team
Goal of leader	Get to the top, be successful	Help the team outperform rivals
Leader's performance	Equals leader's career success	Depends on team's performance
Subordinates' roles	Help the leader succeed	Unite in the pursuit of shared goal
Key leader attributes	Confidence and charisma	Competence and integrity

As a consequence, organizations often assume that a leader's career success reflects his or her performance—the more senior a leader, the more talented the person must be.

To judge leaders' talent, we need to objectively consider their teams' performance. Objective assessment, however, can be confounded by a shortage of comparative cases, the existence of confounding factors, or simply noisy or insufficient data. But despite these challenges, organizations must still try to assess team performance. Failing that, we can look at team morale as a good proxy because it is both a cause and a consequence of higher team performance and because teams know how their leaders behave. Moreover, subordinates' goal isn't to help their leaders attain greater personal success; they want to pursue a common goal, which the leader must facilitate. Clearly, the leader traits that work toward this common goal are not confidence or charisma, but rather competence and integrity.

CHAPTER 7

Learning to Distrust Our Instincts

I spend a great deal of my time trying to teach organizations how to identify better leaders. Although you would think that organizations—particularly large multinationals—are quite sophisticated in their leadership selection practices, a quick interaction with their leaders shows that this is certainly not the case. Here's a recent conversation I had with a senior executive of a top investment bank:

> *Me:* How do you know if someone has potential for leadership?
>
> *Bank executive:* Well, you just know!
>
> *Me:* What exactly do you mean?
>
> *Bank executive:* You know, I just know it when I see it.

If this attitude exists in one of the largest and most successful organizations in the world, what can we expect from more run-of-the-mill companies?

In a recent study I conducted with the Corporate Research Forum, a boutique think tank, 75 percent of HR leaders from top global companies reported that the most common approach for determining that someone has leadership potential is the subjective opinion of the person's boss.[1] Given that organizations are interested in at least seeming objective, we can only imagine that the real rate of intuitive decisions is even higher.

Why such reliance on intuition? Few organizations are good at measuring leaders' performance. Although organizations often obsess over identifying leadership potential, they rarely bother checking whether their choices end up being right.

And yet once organizations understand what qualities they should be looking for, they should have little difficulty detecting these qualities. Contrary to common belief, robust methods for identifying leadership potential have been around for decades, and there are very simple criteria to test whether they work. But therein lies the problem: we love to trust our instincts, even when they're wrong.

As is hopefully clear by now, organizations often choose the wrong leaders. Why don't they realize that their methods are flawed? For one reason, people evaluating the leaders are the same people hiring and promoting them. The most common example of this arrangement is when candidates who are hired on the basis of their interview performance are later evaluated by the same people who appointed them. That is, an interviewer makes a bad decision and is later asked to verify whether the decision was right. In such situations, the hiring manager doesn't even have to consciously cheat to conceal the earlier mistake. The same biases that lead managers to hire the wrong candidate in the first place will continue to contaminate their evaluations of the candidate's performance once he or she is on the job. And all this will be exacerbated even further when objective facts about the candidate's performance are hard to obtain (or easy to ignore or misinterpret).

The design flaws that contaminate organizational judgments of leadership potential apply to both men and women, though the balance of the evidence shows that women end up being more disadvantaged than men. Many articles and books have summed up this research, but put simply, women are punished for displaying many traits regarded as central to leadership emergence. Ambition, risk-taking, assertiveness, and other similar traits are frowned on in women because they are stereotypically masculine. And yet when a woman fails to display such traits—meaning she behaves in traditionally feminine ways—she is easily dismissed for not being leader-like.[2]

Take Hillary Clinton, who during the last presidential election was repeatedly criticized for being cold, ambitious, unemotional, and robotic. Even if these adjectives accurately described Clinton's persona, they would have had a much less negative connotation if they had been associated with a man. In fact, when was the last time that male leaders were accused of being any of these things, and when did such an accusation hurt their leadership prospects? At the same time, the only alternative for Clinton was to be categorized as a woman, which was unavoidable, given that she was the first female candidate ever to be nominated for president by a major party. But her being a woman meant that she was also attacked for being weak and lacking in stamina. Clearly, then, women face a catch-22 to confront the pervasive biases underlying people's stereotype of a good leader. When they display stereotypically masculine traits, women are dismissed for not being a typical woman; when they display stereotypically feminine traits, women are dismissed for not being a typical leader. Consequently, women need to be more qualified than men do, to compete with men for the same leadership roles.[3]

To overcome these biases and hire the right leaders, organizations need to put in place solid metrics for evaluating leadership performance, minimizing their reliance on subjective judgments. A leader's performance is the sum of actions that lead to the achievement of organizational goals, and objective measures of the leader's performance enable an organization to determine whether its leadership selection process actually works. If you don't know what you are doing wrong, you cannot improve, except through sheer luck.

Measuring intellectual capital, or the problem with interviews

What key signals should organizations focus on if they want to detect true leadership potential? The first type of signal concerns intellectual capital, which, as described earlier, comprises the candidate's expertise, knowledge, and formal credentials. The most common vehicle for assessing intellectual capital is the curriculum vitae, résumé, LinkedIn profile, or online portfolio. Emphasis on intellectual capital will continue to decrease as focus on psychological capital grows, but there's no doubt that intellectual capital still matters, in particular to weed out unqualified candidates. Leaders need to be credible with their subordinates, and technical skills and hard expertise provide credibility.

Another common approach to evaluating intellectual capital is the selection interview. Regardless of the job, industry, or type and size of an organization, the leadership identification process will always include an interview, and usually more than one. Furthermore, job interviews are often the only way that organizations evaluate external candidates for a leadership role. And even when used in conjunction with other tools, interviews are likely to have more weight than other measures do. If candidates excel in other selection criteria but do poorly on the interview, they will probably not be selected.

Given the universality of the interview, there is a wealth of data on the accuracy and utility of interviews as predictors of performance, with no fewer than fifteen meta-analyses and hundreds of independent studies published.[4] These studies show that *structured* interviews are a robust method for vetting leaders' potential. Structured interviews contain a predefined scoring template to pick up job-relevant signals. They are tightly linked to key job requirements and use standardized scoring templates to minimize irrelevant signals (e.g., confidence, charisma, and sense of humor). Here are some examples of structured-interview questions:

> *Technical expertise:* Have you used Excel before? Are you familiar with the Python software? Can you give business development presentations in French?

> *Leadership skills:* On a scale from 1 to 10, where 6 is the average, how would you rate your ability to manage a virtual team? Do you have any experience leading innovation teams? Is your leadership style more hands-on or hands-off?

Crucially, in structured interviews, all candidates are asked the same questions in the same order, and hiring managers are trained to interpret answers in a consistent manner.

Whereas structured interviews vet candidates' potential more objectively and hence effectively, unstructured interviews predict job performance less accurately.[5] First, the open-ended questions invite unexpected responses that are hard to interpret and analyze. Second, the questions are asked in any order and without a predefined model, and the answers cannot be linked to specific competencies or job requirements. The unstructured interview is more of an improvised and free-floating exercise, where interviewers invite candidates to present themselves on different questions—some mere icebreakers, some tricky—and their performance is judged spontaneously. Here are some examples of unstructured interview questions:

> Did you have any trouble finding us?
>
> Why do you want to work for us?
>
> How did you find working for your previous employer?
>
> Do you have any hobbies?
>
> Where do you see yourself in five years?
>
> What are your biggest weaknesses?

Unsurprisingly, unstructured interviews increase conscious and unconscious biases about candidates, and selections are often based on job-irrelevant qualities (e.g., race, gender, and age). No matter how willing an interviewer is to ignore these factors, he or she cannot avoid taking them into account. Psychological studies have shown that the more we attempt to ignore some thoughts, the more prominently those very thoughts feature in our mind. Try not to think of a white bear, and the only thing in your mind will be a white bear.[6] Try to ignore a candidate's nationality, ethnicity, or gender, and you will almost certainly fail to ignore it. Besides, as shown in chapter 4, we tend to form views on people after just a few milliseconds of interaction, and even candidates' handshakes influence interviewers' decisions, albeit unconsciously.[7]

In a recent study, Iris Bohnet from Harvard's Kennedy School of Government and her team underscored the benefit of structured evaluations of leadership. They found that when interviewers compare different candidates on the same competencies—looking at the group against each key criterion—the interviewers are more likely to evaluate the candidates' potential accurately and arrive at rational and unbiased hiring decisions, escaping the influence of gender stereotypes. Structured interviews, particularly standardized comparisons and evaluations of candidates, will therefore help minimize biases. In contrast, when interviewers focused on one candidate at a time, separately discussing each individual's performance, they fell back on gendered heuristics, inadvertently relying on social stereotypes (e.g., men are ambitious and smart, and women are warm and conscientious). Thus, unstructured interviews, and the subjective ways they are evaluated, activate interviewers' biases.[8]

Measuring psychological capital, or the upside of assessments

The best and most accurate measures of psychological capital are psychometric tests, which come in two kinds:

intelligence tests and personality inventories.[9] Intelligence tests are usually timed and focus on measuring leaders' general reasoning, problem-solving skills, and broad thinking skills. They are generally classified as measures of learning ability or IQ and represent the best measure of leaders' raw mental horsepower. Although these tests may often seem too abstract to relate to everyday work problems, they are without doubt the best single predictor of job performance, and they remain a useful indicator of leadership potential even when other tools and data are taken into account. Intelligence tests are also highly cost-effective, with many high-quality tests costing less than $30 per candidate.

Of course, these tests are not perfect. First, candidates may underperform on them because of anxiety, which is particularly likely when their tests results have high-stakes implications, as in the case of executive selection. Psychological studies have shown that merely writing candidates' names with red ink, a color known to elicit anxiety, decreases candidates' test performance. Second, intelligence tests can have an adverse impact on minority groups. Ironically, these tests were created to increase meritocracy and help people with more potential be selected for jobs, yet more often than not, they will exacerbate existing social injustices. Intelligence tests are also worse predictors of leadership than employee performance is, partly because there is less variability in intelligence scores at higher levels on the organizational ladder. Employees are often (though not always) selected into leadership roles on the basis of their intelligence.

Personality inventories evaluate people's default behavioral tendencies—how they differ from other people in their reactions to situations—as well as people's core values and beliefs. As already noted, personality has bright-side and dark-side components, or desirable and undesirable tendencies, respectively. When personality assessments are scientifically validated, they will assess five broad areas of the bright side, namely, extraversion, agreeableness, conscientiousness, neuroticism, and openness to experience.[10] Labels may change, and some traits represent narrow facets of these five major personality traits. For example, optimism is part of extraversion, the striving for achievement is part of conscientiousness, and stress tolerance is part of neuroticism. Other traits, such as EQ, represent combinations of the main five factors (i.e., low neuroticism and high extraversion, agreeableness, conscientiousness, and openness to experience). Although certain scores are usually better than others for leadership potential, most personality assessments allow organizations to customize the scoring algorithms to identify the qualities that make for effective leadership in a particular role, culture, or context.

A common criticism of personality assessments is that because they are generally based on self-reports, they can be easily gamed by candidates, particularly if the results have high-stake implications. However, this criticism is largely unfounded. When personality assessments are appropriately designed and validated, it is hard for candidates to spot the right answers.

First, candidates cannot easily infer what each question is evaluating, and in the unlikely event that they can, they cannot necessarily guess what the organizations are looking for in a specific role. Many questions may seem obvious to the candidate, but that doesn't mean that he or she knows how to answer. For example, candidates who agree with the statement "people are quick to recognize my talents" receive lower EQ scores but higher narcissism scores, because people who agree with that statement tend to behave arrogantly and act entitled—behavior indicative of low rather than high EQ.

Second, even when candidates do game the assessment, it still works. The ability to identify the right answers is usually positively correlated with future job performance. As a result, whether candidates have faked their answers or answered genuinely, the results are meaningful as long as their answers still predict performance. Personality assessments in leader selection have a pragmatic purpose: to predict leadership performance, not to solve the metaphysical question of whether candidates truly mean what they say, or whether scores reflect a leader's "true self." As long as the test predicts performance, the question of honesty has less relevance. After all, lots of us—even the sincerest among us—are often not honest with ourselves, and even self-deluded.

Personality assessments are also used to evaluate leaders' values, particularly because many leaders who are potentially able to perform well may be a poor fit for the specific role or organization's culture. But if organizations want leaders to drive change, they would be well advised to hire moderate misfits rather than candidates who are a perfect fit for the current culture. A carbon copy of the rest of the team could perpetuate rather than disrupt the status quo. At the same time, hiring people who are radically different will rarely generate the desired change. More likely, these leaders would end up disrupting only themselves.

Leaders' values operate as their inner compass, dictating not only what they will like, dislike, reward, and sanction, but also the type of culture and climate they will try to create in their teams and organizations. Their values also establish what type of people they will try to hire. Consciously or not, people always prefer to hire candidates who are similar to them in values.

Knowing a leader's values is pointless unless organizations can also decode their own values, or what we call culture. Sadly, because most organizations underestimate the importance of accurately profiling their culture, they end up relying on intuitive and unrealistic ideas that say more about what they would like to be than about what they actually are.[11] For example, many companies today describe themselves as entrepreneurial, innovative, results-oriented, or diverse, even though their own employees may experience a very different culture. Well-designed climate surveys, which crowdsource people's views and experiences of the organizational culture, reveal a company's true values much better than do the aspirational competencies curated by senior executives.

Of course, some leaders manage to perform well in virtually any context. Their ability to span a range of competing competencies makes them more versatile. But they are an exception rather than the norm. In contrast, most people's leadership potential will depend somewhat on the situation; there is no guarantee that a person will lead effectively just because he or she has been effective in a previous role or organization.[12]

Measuring new talent signals, or the promise of new technologies

There has been much innovation in talent-identification tools over the past few years, mostly because of the digital revolution, including the now near-universal adoption of smartphones. When an organization is faced with decisions about people, reputation is the most important data point it can hope to have. The importance of reputation, of course, is nothing new. Rewind back to ancient times, in particular when our ancestors lived in small groups and had frequent, close interactions with one another. At that time, reputation was the definitive currency for social interaction. People knew very well whom to trust and distrust, and it was simple for them to judge other people's talents and, consequently, to pick the right leaders.

However, in an age when we are habitually forced to interact with strangers and to regularly make high-stake decisions about people we barely know, technology and brands have supplanted firsthand experience as the main vehicle for capturing and communicating people's reputation. Inevitably, this move away from the personal to the technical has implications for the leadership identification industry.

Data is making it easier to find, vet, and fit leaders for particular roles, or at least faster and cheaper. Although technological advances in leadership identification are still in their infancy, several innovations promise to upgrade an organization's ability to find better leaders and disrupt the talent-identification industry in the process. In particular, we can look to the contribution of the following technological innovations for finding new signals of talent or potential.

Workforce analytics

Since we spend most of our working hours online, we are leaving behind a rich digital footprint encapsulating a vast repertoire of behaviors, preferences, and thoughts. Some organizations will therefore assess talent by monitoring and measuring day-to-day employee activities, uncovering new signals for potential, engagement, and performance.

Large call centers are pioneers in this area. For years, they have tracked the number of calls and breaks employees take, how many customer problems they solve, and the satisfaction ratings customers leave. In the future, technology will make it easy for organizations to deploy a similar approach in a wide range of jobs, including managerial and leadership roles.

For instance, companies will be able to use email traffic to predict sales and profits and to measure a team's level of engagement, which is a very direct and reliable metric of how the team's leader is performing. Tracking daily behavior generates enormous quantities of data—more than a human being could possibly interpret—so organizations will increasingly rely on algorithms to extract individual, team, and organizational diagnostics from their in-house data. Although some employees may object to having their data mined by algorithms, the technological approach makes sense for at least two reasons. First, employees' email traffic and other work-related data are legitimate sources of information that signal how employees are performing. After all, work is what employees should be doing. Second, even if such signals are imperfect, they are likely to be more accurate and less biased when analyzed by computer-generated algorithms than by human managers, who have their own agendas and are often unable to keep a close eye on everyone's performance.

Web scraping

Organizations will also use algorithms to mine people's external data, translating their web and social media activity into a quantitative estimate of their job potential or talent. Research beginning around 2012 indicates that this methodology, broadly known as *web scraping*, can help employers obtain a reliable estimate of employees' IQ and personality.[13] Candidates' digital footprints include information that they have deliberately collected and curated—such as LinkedIn endorsements and recommendations—but also comments, photos, and videos posted by colleagues, clients, friends, and family on less professional platforms, such as Facebook or Instagram.

As we might expect, there are now several businesses, such as Reputation.com, to help leaders not just monitor, but also clean up their online images. Clearly, web scraping has ethical and legal implications, particularly when firms request applicants' social media passwords as part of the vetting process. Enough companies have made such requests of their applicants that at least twenty-three US states have introduced or considered legislation to ban the practice. Meanwhile, the European Union has introduced a strict policy—the General Data Protection Regulation—to constrain companies' ability to mine digital records without consumers' consent. Although there is now a clear difference between what we could and should know about candidates, today we can easily gather digital records on people without trampling on privacy rights, by explicitly asking them to opt in or consent to having their data analyzed. If candidates see a potential advantage, such as improving their job situation or demonstrating their talents, in having their data analyzed, a large group of candidates might allow these AI algorithms to translate the data they have already given away for "free" (mostly for marketing purposes) into a useful career enhancer. For example, if my Facebook data suggest that I'm an extravert, I may consider a career in sales or PR. Or if my tweets indicate that I'm highly curious, I may look into jobs that provide more learning opportunities. Or if my Spotify playlist reveals emotional volatility, I may consider some coaching or anger management before accepting that leadership job offer.

Gamification

In the context of assessing potential, *gamification* means creating IQ or personality tests that are fun to take—or at least more enjoyable than traditional assessment tools, which have historically been long and boring. Participants solve puzzles or complete challenges to earn points and badges. The goal of enhancing user experience like this is to increase response rates. By offering free, entertaining tests online—and providing instant developmental feedback—companies can attract many thousands of engaged test takers.

Reckitt Benckiser, Red Bull, and Deloitte are a few of the global firms that have relied on gamified assessments to evaluate potential candidates, particularly millennials. Developers still have some work to do to bridge the gap between fun and accuracy—and gamified tests are usually more expensive to create and administer than the typical questionnaire, especially if they manage to combine the look and feel of video games with the accuracy of scientific assessments. Even so, employers are keenly interested in this entertaining testing technology because it can help identify more people with high potential by reaching beyond the applicant pool, effectively marketing the organization as a workplace that's fun.

Smart badges

Humanyze, an MIT spin off led by Ben Waber, who coined the term *people analytics*, tags employees and leaders with sensors that capture their movements, communications, and even physiological responses (e.g., stress, excitement, and boredom). Just by analyzing anonymous group-level data, the firm can help organizations identify invisible elements of work relations, such as the hidden power dynamics, in a firm.

For example, in a recent study reported in *Harvard Business Review*, Waber and his team set out to decode the behavioral differences between men and women in a large multinational firm and explore whether such differences could partly explain the underrepresentation of women in the senior leadership ranks (where they accounted for just 20 percent).[14] The researchers gathered email data, meeting schedule data, and location data for hundreds of employees, across all seniority levels, over four months. Of particular relevance was the data collected with sensors some employees wore. The sensors recorded who talked with whom; where, when, and for how long people communicated with each other; and who dominated each conversation. Waber's team expected to find behavioral differences between men and women pertaining to people's drive and networking habits: "Perhaps women had fewer mentors, less face time with managers, or weren't as proactive as men in talking to senior leadership." However, the results showed no significant differences between what women and men did at work: "Women had the same number of contacts as men, they spent as much time with senior leadership, and they allocated their time similarly to men in the same role. We couldn't see the types of projects they were working on, but we found that men and women had indistinguishable work patterns in the amount of time they spent online, in concentrated work, and in face-to-face conversation. And in performance evaluations men and women received statistically identical scores. This held true for women at each level of seniority. Yet women weren't advancing and men were."

Clearly, then, at least in this organization, there are no justifiable reasons for the uneven proportion of men and women in senior leadership. If men and women behave in the same way and perform in the same way, the only explanation for the higher success rates of men is that they are given preferential treatment. Importantly, technology enables organizations to capture and crunch data at the most granular level of everyday behaviors to demonstrate what may otherwise seem a matter of subjective opinion.

Network analysis

While network analysis is still not widely used to identify leadership potential, it should be. Network analysis looks at who people email, how often they communicate, and when, as well as how many active connections people work with, both internally and externally. The data from this analysis can also reveal where people go when they need expertise or other help. Interestingly, network analysis can reveal significant gaps between who the official leaders are and who is informally exercising leadership in the organization. For instance, research has shown that there is little overlap between individuals who are acting as the main agents of innovation—by generating ideas and proactively translating creative initiatives into actual innovations—and those with a formal innovation leadership role.[15] Moreover, many senior leaders are too isolated from the central networks of the organization to exert the level of influence that is expected of them. In the future, organizations may use social network analysis not just to visualize the dynamics of interaction, but also for internal leadership identification, particularly if they are interested in unearthing some hidden gems.

In an age where nearly half of the world is online and daily iPhone sales outpace human births, there are few limits to the potential of digital talent tools, particularly as more and more people are depositing a significant portion of their lives online. But to fulfill even a fraction of this potential, these novel AI-based tools must meet legal and ethical standards and be sufficiently accurate. If the tools can meet these requirements, then organizations will benefit from a much deeper and wider access to talent, including the ability to attract and hire better leaders.

CHAPTER **8**

How Leaders
Get Better

By any measure, John was a terrible leader. Most of his direct reports disrespected him and hated working from him. The rest were indifferent, but since he provided them with no direction or feedback, they were clueless about their jobs and consequently underperformed. Predictably, his team was consistently ranked at the bottom on every indicator of performance—including sales, productivity, innovation, and profits—except turnover. Indeed, only people who were unable to find alternatives ended up working for John for longer than a couple of years, and they did so purely because they had little choice. One of the main reasons for John's problem was his own personality. Neither particularly smart nor hardworking, he had poor people skills and rarely accepted his mistakes. As a matter of fact, John saw himself as a terrific leader. He rated his own performance highly and seemed utterly blind to the very problems he had created.

Fortunately, his boss persuaded him to start working with a coach. After merely a few weeks, John started changing his bad behaviors, providing clear objectives and feedback to his team, becoming self-critical, and making smarter decisions. The transformation was so great that his team became instantly aware of the change, to the point of perceiving him as a completely different leader and person. As a result, John's team started to perform much better. People's engagement levels rose, turnover dropped to zero while sales, productivity, and profits skyrocketed. John's reputation as one of the best bosses in the organization spread, and suddenly, the most talented and ambitious people in the firm wanted to work for him, or at least emulate his winning leadership formula.

Stories like this are so unbelievable that they don't even feature in fictional accounts of leadership. And yes, our friend John is total fiction. Think about this: we have inspirational stories—both real and imaginary—of people who went from extreme poverty to mega wealth, from alarming sickness to obsessive health freaks, and from ignorance to wisdom. However, we don't even bother making up stories of bosses who went from terrible to amazing. If we did, they would probably be classified as science fiction. In contrast, and as earlier chapters have demonstrated, there is no shortage of real-life examples for leaders who were great until they deteriorated. The pathway from good to bad seems much easier than the one going from bad to good.

Leadership development for the win

No matter how good an organization is at spotting and attracting individuals with leadership potential, the individuals must be able to turn this potential into action. Perhaps more importantly, when an organization is not particularly good at uncovering leadership potential in people and doesn't select its leaders for their potential, the organization must invest in leadership development. A recent survey of twenty-five hundred business and HR leaders found that 86 percent of organizations consider leadership development either very important or an urgent priority.[1]

Many organizations trust in leaders' ability to get better. Consider that 80 percent of talent management budgets are typically devoted to learning, training, and development interventions, and the big bulk of that outlay is reserved for leaders. Michael Beer at Harvard Business School estimates that organizations around the world are spending over $360 billion each year on programs to improve the performance of their people.[2] He notes that despite this huge investment, organizations fail to accomplish the desired improvements in their leaders, particularly when top leadership is not fully committed to change.

Although it would be nice to develop every employee, interventions on leaders can be expected to have the highest ROI. Leaders affect so many people, processes, and outcomes, any improvements to leadership will spill over to the rest of the organization and wider workforce.[3] As the famous Pareto principle states, in any group or organization, only a few individuals—usually no more than 20 percent—will account for at least 80 percent of collective output or productivity, and aside from rare exceptions, those vital few will be leaders.

And yet, the average or typical leadership development intervention fails to produce reliable measures of change, particularly in the form of key performance indicators. Remarkably, meta-analytic reviews suggest that many interventions produce no results, and quite a few produce *negative* results, actually worsening leaders' performance.[4] A comprehensive review of organizational feedback—arguably the single most important feature in any leadership development intervention—suggests that 30 percent of the time, feedback ends up making leaders less effective than they were originally.[5] Most shocking of all, there is a strong negative correlation between the money spent on interventions to improve the quality of leadership and people's confidence in their leaders.[6]

Six data-driven lessons in leadership development

Going from leadership incompetence to leadership competence is not easy, but compelling evidence attests to the efficacy of well-designed, albeit rare, leadership development programs. So, some programs do work. But their effectiveness is built on making leaders aware of their limitations, persuading them to replace their toxic habits with more effective ones, and linking those habits to critical business performance metrics. There *are* ways of doing it right, and helping leaders improve can make organizations more effective. That said, we need to be aware of the constraints and barriers that make substantial improvements difficult. Here are six lessons from science.

1. Some characteristics are hard to change

Like any human quality, leadership talent comes from developmental experiences. Think of sports and athletic ability as a comparison. In principle, anyone can become a good athlete, but that doesn't mean that the probability of becoming a good athlete is the same for everyone. The same goes for leadership and other psychological traits. For example, intelligence, which, as seen in chapter 7, is a key ingredient of leadership talent, would never develop without appropriate environmental stimulation.[7] Deprive smart children from mental stimulation, and they will almost certainly grow up less advanced intellectually than they would if given such stimulation. At the same time, early manifestations of intelligence reliably predict how smart a person becomes later in life.[8] How much smarter you are than others at age fifty can be predicted quite accurately from the same comparison at age five, and there are relatively few changes to the ranking at both ages.

Many key developmental experiences that shape people's leadership potential occur very early in life, certainly before individuals arrive at the office or are considered for leadership positions. In that sense, William Wordsworth's line "The Child is Father of the Man" rightly applies. The most logical answer to arguably the most popular question in leadership—are leaders born or made?—is yes. As a scientist wisely observed, "Asking how much a particular individual's attitudes or traits are due to heredity versus the environment is nonsensical, just like asking whether a leaky basement is caused more by the crack in the foundation or the water outside."[9]

Like any other personality trait, leadership is part nature and part nurture. We understand this duality of origins from behavioral genetic studies. Research that compared fraternal twins (who share 50 percent of their DNA) with identical twins (who share 100 percent of their DNA) on their leadership measures found that leadership scores increase with genetic similarity.[10] Although leadership is far less heritable than height (90 percent) or weight (80 percent), around 30 percent of leadership potential is determined by genetic factors.[11] While this lower percentage attributed to "nature" may seem like good news for both the leadership development industry and individuals hoping to boost their leadership talents, we still don't necessarily understand or control the remaining 70 percent that is "nurture." In fact, we are much better at predicting than boosting leadership performance. If we want an animal to climb a tree, we are better off finding a squirrel than training a fish.

When AT&T pioneered leadership assessment and development centers in the 1970s, putting hundreds of leaders through highly structured and standardized programs, the company assessed the relative impact of training and talent on subsequent leadership performance. The main finding? Leadership effectiveness was highly predictable; the rank order of leaders' performance remained remarkably unchanged before and after training. Training was not irrelevant but, rather, did little to alter the existing performance differences between people. In the same vein, a recent meta-analysis investigated which aspects of a person's job performance could be attributed to deliberate practice and training.[12] The researchers looked at various fields and professions and found that training had the greatest effect in areas where the rules are clear, performance can be measured objectively, and improvisation is minimal. Nevertheless, in all fields, training had only a minor effect on job performance: 26 percent for games, 21 percent for music, 18 percent for sports, 4 percent for education, and just 1 percent for the average profession.

In comparison, simply evaluating where leaders stand on the general dimensions of personality—the big five—accounted for around 50 percent of the variability in leadership emergence and effectiveness, meaning that half of your success as a leader is dictated by your personality. Furthermore, whereas it takes a great deal of time and effort to change even the smallest of personal habits, personality can be evaluated rapidly with standardized assessments that can be administered remotely in less than forty-five minutes.[13]

In fact, recent research suggests that we don't even need to put leaders through a formal assessment to predict their performance. A team of economists at the University of Chicago Booth School of Business used phone call data from earnings calls to infer the personality of CEOs. For example, extraverted CEOs used more words per minute and spoke more energetically, conscientious CEOs provided more detail and factual information, and so on. This passive—and no doubt imperfect—measure of personality predicted a significant chunk of the variability in firms' financial performance (e.g., cash flow, return on assets, and profitability).[14]

2. Good coaching works

Even if prediction trumps development, there's little doubt that well-designed coaching programs do work. Sadly, few organizations have a rigorous process in place to evaluate the ROI of coaching, and the growing body of scientific evidence provides inadequate insight, because interventions are so different and because few people know what really happens behind closed doors during a coaching session.[15] Fundamentally, coaching is not pure science. It is partly an art, which explains the huge variability in effectiveness between different coaches. The success of coaching will largely depend on the talent and skill of the coach, and individual coaches' characteristics and behaviors have been found to matter more than does the coaching method.[16]

The most common intervention to improve the performance of leaders is executive coaching, which consists of one-on-one sessions between a coach and a leader. Unlike the goal in psychological therapy, the goal in leadership coaching is not just to deal with problematic habits but also to support the development of critical leadership competencies to make the leader more effective. Coaches and leaders will typically identify a range of behaviors that the leader ought to start, stop, or keep doing to improve his or her performance, and these improvements should translate into better team performance.

Many coaching interventions focus on enhancing people's EQ, though often under the label of social, intrapersonal, interpersonal, or soft skills.[17] The coaches aim to make leaders more approachable and easier to deal with—not a bad strategy for improving their performance, since the key problems that leaders must solve are ultimately people problems. As the clever aphorism, sometimes attributed to Oscar Wilde, goes, "Some cause happiness wherever they go; others whenever they go." EQ training is particularly useful for leaders in the latter category.

While no intervention can boost a leader's EQ (or indeed any other competency) from 0 to 100 percent, competent coaching programs can be expected to produce average improvements of 25 percent. Tim Theeboom and his colleagues at the University of Amsterdam published a seminal meta-analysis in this area, reviewing forty-six independent studies on coaching effects. They found that 70 percent of the individuals who were coached could be expected to outperform those who weren't.[18] Key EQ areas that coaching could improve included coping skills, stress management, and self-regulation, the last of which is a core component of motivation and affects how leaders set and achieve their goals. Even more biological aspects of EQ, such as empathy, turn out to be somewhat coachable. For instance, neuropsychological studies suggest that, with adequate coaching, people can become more prosocial, altruistic, and compassionate and that such changes will be visible in brain imaging studies.[19]

The most successful coaching sessions focus on changing leaders' behaviors. Effective leader behavior is, of course, a prerequisite for improving any organizational outcomes under a leader's influence.[20] After all, a leader's thinking is less critical than what he or she actually does. Good coaching, then, helps leaders replace counterproductive behaviors with more effective ones. For example, if leaders tend to micromanage their staff, they may want to develop the habit of giving people more autonomy. Conversely, if leaders understand that they are too hands-off with their subordinates, they may coach themselves to be more hands-on, providing their reports with clear instructions and feedback and monitoring people's performance more closely. All these approaches strongly contrast with the belief that leaders will improve more by focusing on what they are already doing well, that is, by focusing on their strengths.

3. Beware of leaders' strengths

Since the new century, few coaching approaches have enjoyed as much popularity as has *strengths coaching*, which posits that instead of worrying about their flaws, leaders should concentrate on enhancing their positive qualities. Strengths coaching has a cult-like following in many HR departments, and Amazon lists over eight thousand books on the topic. Among these is Gallup's best-selling *StrengthsFinder*, which is reportedly used by 1.6 million employees across *Fortune* 500 companies every year.[21]

Although it is no doubt easier to get better at the tasks we are already good at, particularly if we like those tasks (e.g., giving presentations, strategizing, business development, and giving feedback), we ignore our limitations at our own peril, especially if we want to get better. In fact, negative feedback—feedback that highlights a deficit in potential or performance—is the most useful type. It highlights the gap between where leaders are and where they should be.[22] Furthermore, assuming that leaders would benefit from developing new strengths—competencies they do not presently possess—then there is no room for strengths-based interventions.

Finally, everything is better in moderation; the only exception is moderation itself. Even positive qualities have adverse effects when taken to the extreme. For instance, attention to detail can become counterproductive perfectionism and excessive procrastination. Confidence may turn into arrogance, risk-taking, and hubris. Ambition may become greed, and imagination may turn into eccentricity. Strengths may especially overdevelop in this way when we select leaders with these characteristics and place the people in environments that exacerbate these tendencies.

4. Self-awareness is essential

Self-awareness, the cornerstone of leadership development, has been valued for thousands of years. The entrance to the temple of Apollo in Delphi was inscribed *know thyself.* Socrates argued that the essence of his wisdom was to accept his ignorance. Given that people are generally unaware of their limitations, which are exacerbated when they become leaders, leadership development interventions should focus on boosting leaders' self-awareness. Research suggests that greater self-awareness is a defining feature of high-performing leaders.[23] Accordingly, because good coaching enhances the person's self-awareness, coaching is often described as systematic feedback.[24]

People need feedback to enhance their self-awareness and gain more insights into their own strengths and weaknesses, but when feedback is unclear or inaccurate, it will do more harm than good. Similarly, if feedback only tells leaders what they want to hear or what they already know, it will have no impact on their performance (even if the feedback clear and accurate).

Unfortunately, we are not naturally predisposed to seeking feedback, either at work or in other situations. This is particularly true when it comes to negative feedback: have

you ever worked for a boss who would occasionally ask
you, "What am I doing wrong?" or "How could I have
done this better?"? Most people have not.

Why, then, do leaders hesitate to receive feedback?
First, leaders are generally overconfident, so they interpret
their actions more favorably than they should. Second,
in most cultures—especially the Western world—seeking
feedback is seen as a sign of weakness. Indeed, there is
a natural tension between performing and learning, and
most leaders are too focused on the former to care about
the latter. It takes some humility to accept that we have
something to learn, and leaders are generally disinterested
in exposing their limitations, even when they are aware
of them.

All these factors prompt organizations to use data–driven
tools, such as 360-degree assessments and personality
reports, to facilitate developmental feedback for leaders.
A controlled experimental study of 1,361 global corpo-
ration managers showed that feedback-based coaching
increased the managers' propensity to seek advice and
improved their subsequent performance one year later.[25]

5. It is not easy to go against our nature

Despite the overwhelming number of decisions we make
every day and the absolute certainty most of us feel about
the control we have over those choices, we also act rather
predictably, even when our decisions appear rationally
planned.[26] Human predictability is less surprising when we

examine the behavior of other people. Accordingly, our own behavior will also seem less surprising to others. It is not that we cannot change, but rather, we are not as committed to making those changes as we ought to be. As the popular saying goes, "Everybody wants to go to heaven, but nobody wants to die." We don't want to change—we want to *have changed*. Sure, we can all make a wide range of decisions in any given situation, but even when we are free to make such decisions, more often than not our choices are quite predictable.

Most of the habits that define us have been cemented over many years, and they are equally slow to be abandoned or changed. Consider that the average New Year's resolution is broken within the first months, even though it concerns concrete and measurable aspects of behavior that we truly want to change and the change depends entirely on us.[27] Clearly, things will be even more challenging when we have to change something we are not particularly desperate to change, when the change itself depends on many other factors, and when the results are harder to judge. There's no point in knowing where you want to go if you are unable to work out whether you got there.

Most people report that they would like to change some aspect of their personality. For instance, research shows that at any age, around 80 percent of people are eager to boost their emotional stability, extraversion, agreeableness, openness to experience, or conscientiousness; such improvements would equate to enhancing their EQ and, in turn, their leadership potential.[28] At the same time, studies suggest that we can expect to see two main personality changes in most people, even if people are not engaged in deliberate change interventions.[29]

First, as people grow older they tend to become slightly more boring versions of their younger selves. Their agreeableness and conscientiousness goes up, but their openness to new experiences goes down. We call this change *psychological maturity*, but it's really a euphemism for *boring*.

Second, when leaders change, they tend to become more exaggerated versions of themselves. *Niche picking*, the psychological principle that explains this tendency, concerns our natural inclination to seek out experiences that are a good fit for our personality. When we do look for these familiar, preferred activities, our proclivities are strengthened. For example, extraverted leaders will seek out situations in which they can connect with new people, be the center of attention, and behave in more upbeat and energetic ways, and those situations will, in turn, make those leaders more upbeat and energetic and better at both connecting with others and performing as the center of attention.

To summarize, most leaders are already programmed to play to their strengths, and they do that quite well. Effective development will need to counterbalance this tendency, to help leaders go against their nature and go to places they would not have gone. In the words of motivational speaker Zig Ziglar, "You don't change your decision to go—you do change your direction to get there."[30]

6. Coachability is an integral part of potential

Paradoxically, coaching is most helpful for those who need it the least. Indeed, different people will benefit differently from coaching and other leader development interventions. For example, leaders' curiosity determines the degree to which they will seek out developmental feedback or experiences that enable them to increase their skills and expertise. Whenever organizations make available learning and development programs for wide adoption, those who opt in are usually less likely to need them, and those who do need it tend not to opt in.

When leaders are lucky enough get accurate feedback on their potential or performance, they are not always receptive to it. People who are more humble, empathetic, and self-aware will be more likely to capitalize on critical feedback and translate it into self-awareness gains.[31] Conversely—just imagine trying to coach Vladimir Putin or Silvio Berlusconi—individuals who are overconfident, narcissistic, and lacking in empathy will be immune to even the most helpful developmental feedback, so they would probably not benefit from it. Moreover, even when leaders seek out development opportunities and internalize feedback, leaders will only make positive changes if persuaded that they need to get better. As the old joke goes, it only takes one psychologist to change a light bulb, as long as the light bulb really wants to change. Finally, even if leaders want to change, they will need a great deal of willpower and persistence to sustain the behaviors that create more effective habits and a more favorable reputation—and all those qualities are determined by leaders' personalities.

In sum, bad leaders are unlikely to turn into talented, inspirational, or high-performing leaders. Yes, they can change, but most leaders won't improve much beyond what you have seen them do in the past, especially if they are left to their own devices. Human inertia makes professional development interventions, such as executive coaching, indispensable, though a much more effective strategy for improving the quality of leaders would be to focus more time, effort, and resources on selecting talented people into leadership roles. As in any other area, prevention is a much better option than treatment, and while there's no need to choose between one and the other—both should be pursued—leaders will be much more likely to improve when they have been correctly selected.

CHAPTER 9

Measuring a Leader's Impact

When Millard "Mickey" Drexler took over as CEO of Gap in 1983, the iconic American retailer was under great pressure to keep up with a new wave of competitors in the fast-fashion industry. Drexler set out to implement an aggressive turnaround plan that included bold changes. For example, the retailer would no longer sell its competitors' products, in the hope that customers would be happy to switch to the much-higher-margin Gap items. Historically, Gap had mostly been a retailer for Levi's products, with its own products as a secondary feature. This sea change in strategy also repositioned the firm to focus on older and more affluent customers, but the new focus required a total redesign of Gap's clothing line and stores. The new look inspired the later design of the swanky Apple stores. The tech stores had minimal open spaces with plenty of natural light encouraging informal and frequent interactions between staff and customers. The layout nudged customers to interact extensively with the products and stay in the shop for as long as possible. Drexler was on Apple's board of directors and was often described as the "king of retail" or "the Steve Jobs of retail."

Luckily for Gap, Drexler's strategy paid off. In less than two decades after his arrival, the company grew from just $480 million to $13.6 billion in annual sales, and Gap became a central part of American life as well as one of the most admired brands in the world. The stylish, affordable, but casual garments Drexler launched helped prompt a transformation in how Americans dressed at work, and offices around the United States institutionalized casual Fridays to allow employees to dress down ahead of the weekend.

Drexler's transformative impact came as no surprise to those who worked for him. Although he was known for his no-nonsense, blunt style, he commanded respect and admiration from everyone. Few worked as hard as he did, and his hands-on approach to driving growth, combined with his shrewd judgment and expert decision-making and trend-spotting ability, made him a great leader.

And yet, Gap fired Drexler in 2002 amid a decline in growth and revenues, prompting many observers to suggest that he was not the right leader to sustain Gap's long-term success. Although Drexler moved on to become the CEO of J.Crew, where he doubled the company's revenues and transformed the brand into a household name, he eventually stepped down from that job in response to declining sales as well—a repeat of the Gap story.

Although Drexler's story is unique, it also shares something with all other leadership case studies: it is impossible to draw conclusions from a sample size of one person. And, whether a leadership fable is a success or a failure depends on where you put the ending.

Evaluating leaders' impact is still incredibly difficult

Stories *sell*, but data *tells*. So, if we want to understand why certain people are better leaders or whether people are good leaders at all, we need to move beyond individual case studies and in-depth biographical accounts of standout leaders. We have to explore large data sets where hundreds of variables can be examined and manipulated. As psychologist Earl Hunt once noted, "the plural of anecdote is not data."

We need a systematic process and quantitative-analysis tools to mine this extensive data. In the past hundred years, scientists have devoted much time and effort to identifying the key ingredients of leadership talent.[1] The main problem is not a lack of research, but a surplus of it. There is so much information about how the profile of the leader affects teams and organizations that we can become overwhelmed. In contrast, popular blogs and real-world consultants offer memorable anecdotes and catchy formulas that reduce leadership potential to a single overarching competency, a few magic bullet points.

Despite all this focus on leadership success, most leaders remain largely ineffective. Despite multiple reasons for their poor performance, a common theme underlies the various types of leadership incompetence. Namely, leaders have a disconnect between their own individual success and that of the group.

More precisely, traits such as confidence, narcissism, psychopathy, and charisma advance individuals' careers without improving the success of the groups they lead. Clearly, we would be better off if we sifted out individuals with such traits, as opposed to rewarding them. The success of teams and organizations is more important than an individual's personal success, especially when individual victory harms the rest of the group.

But as in the case of Drexler, it's difficult to measure a leader's impact. In fact, it's difficult to measure cause and effect in general. Consider an example of this conundrum in nature. Oxpeckers are often photographed sitting atop large mammals like giraffes and hippos. These colorful African birds seem to embody a classic case of symbiosis, a mutually beneficial relationship. The birds supposedly feed on parasites like ticks, which would otherwise hurt their host animal. But scientists have found that the relationship isn't that simple. Cattle with resident oxpeckers were no more or less likely to have ticks than were cattle without the birds. And researchers noticed that the oxpeckers waited until the ticks were full of blood to eat them—hardly doing the poor mammal any favors. Today, there's still a scientific debate about whether these birds are helpful or harmful to the mammals they sit atop.

Trying to figure out which leaders are good or bad is like trying to figure out whether oxpeckers are helpful or harmful. Is the person sitting atop your organization solving problems—or creating more problems to solve? In the absence of reliable data, it not easy to tell.

Often, we can only see the data clearly after the leaders have left their parasitic footprint on their teams and organizations. And even then, there is no shortage of people who fail to understand the toxic effects of the leader. This is why we see plenty of former politicians and CEOs charging a fortune for after-dinner speeches despite their having ended their former careers in shambles.

Even when we say that an organization is *Darwinian*, there is no guarantee that the outcome of evolution will improve the quality of leaders. For instance, the race to become a CEO or head of state may be a Darwinian process. So is the battle to head a drug cartel. However, just because a contest is brutally competitive does not mean that the survivors will be good for the system. Much like with the oxpeckers, some of the qualities that enable individuals to win these Darwinian battles may not necessarily make them better leaders, because individual fitness may not necessarily translate into group fitness.

Height is an example of this idea in action. In America, a person six feet tall can be expected to earn $200,000 more in their career than someone who is five feet, four inches tall. Yet, few jobs truly require height for better performance. By the same token, height plays a key role in propelling people to leadership positions. A comprehensive review spanning seventy-five years of research shows that height is as strong a predictor of who will become a leader as IQ is—for both men and women.[2] Height is even more consequential in politics. The last time Americans elected a president who was shorter than average was 1896, and in the last hundred years of presidential elections, the shorter of the two final candidates won just 25 percent of the time.

Even if voters perceive taller individuals as more leader-like—a perception that would in turn help tall people become leaders—height, obviously, does not make someone a better leader. Accordingly, height can be helpful to individuals who want to become leaders—especially if they want to become the US president—but groups led by tall people should not expect to be better off than those led by short people. Making height a criterion for selecting a leader would be folly. Nevertheless, trivial traits may sometimes affect results because they are perceived to be important. For example, a team of psychologists led by Elain Wong at the University of Wisconsin correlated the width of CEOs' faces with their companies' earnings: companies led by CEOs with wider faces reported $16 million more in industry-adjusted returns than did companies led by narrower-faced executives. The explanation for these results is that wider faces convey more power and aggressiveness than do narrower faces.[3]

The ever-widening distance between leaders and the rest of us

If we want to understand the present, let alone predict or influence the future, we must remember the past. This recommendation applies to leadership, too. Indeed, several aspects of modern leadership make its assessment a much more complex and difficult enterprise than in the past.

It is impossible to imagine human life without leadership. As long as we and our genetic ancestors have existed, we have always lived in groups, with a person in charge of coordinating our collective activity.[4] This universal function of leaders extends to other species—fish, birds, bees, and so forth. It highlights the evolutionary origins of leadership, the process through which a member of a group guides other members to valuable resources, setting a common goal and direction and aligning the group's efforts with the pursuit of that goal. Thus, leadership evolved as a fundamental mechanism of social coordination that promotes the survival and success of groups. Modern examples of this sort of coordination are high-performing sports teams (e.g., Futbol Club Barcelona), governments (e.g., Singapore's Ministry of Manpower), organizations (e.g., Berkshire Hathaway), and nations (e.g., Sweden).

Today, people often have very little firsthand contact with their leaders. In contrast, thousands of years ago, our hunter-gatherer ancestors lived in small groups that enabled them to have close and frequent interactions with their leaders. The group members knew their leader's reputation and could accurately judge other members' talent and potential for leadership. In addition, these groups were extremely democratic and tended to elect leaders by consensus. As we would expect, this approach led to a high standard of leadership competence, with most chiefs leading through example, reason, and peaceful persuasion. Moreover, these small hunter-gatherer societies were egalitarian, with minimal power differences between men and women and many key duties shared between the sexes.[5]

Fast-forward a few thousand years, and we are living and working in a different world. We work in much larger groups, with minimal physical contact with other group members and leaders. What can a typical McDonald's employee—there are 375,000 of them scattered around 120 countries—say with certainty about their CEO, Steve Easterbrook? How many of them have even heard his name? Likewise, how accurate is the picture that the 1.3 billion citizens of India have of their prime minister, Narendra Modi, if they only see him on TV? To be sure, modern technologies have made it easier to capture information about a leader's reputation—there are YouTube, Facebook, and Glassdoor reviews—but they represent a very noisy and imperfect medium to understand others' potential and cannot substitute for frequent personal contact.

Importantly, our brains have been shaped by millions of years of evolution, so even when our instincts are fueled by outdated models of leadership, it is not easy to *unlearn* them. A century of science has provided an enormous amount of evidence about what good and bad leadership looks like, but this does not erase the archetypes of leadership in our minds. Our gut feel for what constitutes good leadership is shaped much more by our ancestral and evolutionary roots than by the latest leadership research. Environmental changes such as novel work challenges introduced by technology (e.g., virtual teams, a less predictable job landscape, and AI) may call for different leadership qualities, but our implicit models of leadership will not necessarily change quickly.

We have come a long way from the early beginnings of human life, but modern civilization presents new challenges to leaders. The profile of effective leaders today differs from that of our evolutionary past. Even if old models of leadership are no longer effective now, they still match our imaginary leadership archetypes.

How we can do better

Leadership, the process that enables individuals to work together in the pursuit of a common goal, has been a critical resource throughout the evolution of humankind. Every significant accomplishment in human history—the use of fire, the invention of writing, the mapping of the human genome, and so on—sprang from collective action that could not have occurred without leadership.

Whether our goal is to increase the representation of women in leadership or improve the quality of our leaders, we must apply the same solutions: we need to properly understand leadership talent and learn how to measure it. These solutions are easier said than done. Too many decision makers overrate their intuition, and political agendas interfere with the selection of talented leaders, especially when the decision makers are more interested in their own agendas than their organization's well-being. Knowing how to detect true leadership potential is clearly not enough. We also have to introduce measures that place better leaders in key roles and promote a culture that helps them succeed. But without fixing the parameters we use to determine whether someone has talent for leadership, we cannot expect much progress.

As this book has tried to show, organizations can take concrete steps both to improve the performance of their leaders and to increase the representation of women in leadership. They can stop interpreting displays of over-confidence, narcissism, psychopathy, and charisma as signs of leadership potential. They can also acknowledge the importance of EQ, which should be a core competency in any data-driven model of leadership potential. Paying more attention to EQ would augment both the quality of leaders and the number of female leaders, increasing the overall levels of personal effectiveness, self-awareness, and transformational leadership in organizations.

While it is certainly a sign of progress that a growing number of organizations are putting in place deliberate interventions to increase the proportion of women in leadership, a more reasonable goal would be to focus instead on selecting better leaders, as this step would also take care of the gender imbalance. Putting more women in leadership roles does not necessarily improve the quality of leadership, whereas putting more talented leaders into leadership roles will increase the representation of women.

Fundamentally, organizations need to understand that many of the so-called solutions being put in place are making the problem worse. For example, asking women to act more like incompetent men—by self-promoting, faking it, or leaning in when they shouldn't—will only result in the promotion of incompetent women to leadership roles and do very little to correct people's unfair stereotypes of female leaders.

Likewise, any deliberate attempt to introduce formal quotas for an underrepresented group will inevitably convey the impression that such a group is less capable. Why would they need help otherwise? This incorrect assumption is based on the illusion that current systems are meritocratic. We have to challenge this assumption by acknowledging and tackling the politics and nepotism that corrupt the selection of leaders rather than by using positive discrimination.

There is no conflict between boosting gender equality and boosting leadership quality. On the contrary, it is harder to improve the quality of our leaders without increasing the numbers of female leaders.

And yet, the common impression is the reverse, namely, that it would be antimeritocratic to have more women in the higher echelons of the organization. For instance, a 2010 study by Emilio Castilla and Stephen Benard from

MIT's Sloan Business School asked approximately four hundred experienced MBA students to go through an imaginary exercise of bonus allocation.[6] The students were told to allocate $1,000 in bonus money to individual employees according to how those employees were rated by their managers. This process follows mainstream practices in many corporations, where first-line managers evaluate performance but where the allocation of bonuses is made by leaders who inspect these performance evaluations. But there was a twist: half of the students were told that the organization in question was meritocratic, meaning that the goal of bonuses was to reward true performance. Interestingly, the students in this group tended to award higher bonuses to men than to women, even though the men's and women's performance ratings were identical. This uneven allocation was made not just by male students, but also by female students.[7] And we can safely assume that MIT students are significantly more liberal and less gender-biased than the average manager in the business world. To improve the quality of leadership, then, we cannot simply focus on merit. We need to be clearer about the leadership qualities we are looking for: emotional intelligence, intellectual capital, social capital, and psychological capital.

For a recent example, consider Uber, whose former CEO Travis Kalanick had damaged the reputation of the company by allegedly covering up sexual harassment allegations, being caught on camera belittling an Uber driver, and creating an abrasive and ruthless results–driven culture in the organization. The company had tolerated all this damaging behavior before it finally appointed Dara Khosrowshahi, a leader with more stereotypically feminine qualities, in the hope of fixing the company's image and detoxing its culture.

As the *New Yorker* recently noted, "Since joining the company, Khosrowshahi has played the role of flatterer, diplomat, negotiator, and salesman. He was selected by Uber's board in part because of his personality: agreeable, unthreatening, comfortable with the kind of corporate talk that investors find reassuring. Uber's previous CEO, Travis Kalanick, had built the company into an extraordinary success. Under his leadership, it also acquired a terrible reputation."[8]

Although it is too soon to judge Khosrowshahi's performance, Uber no doubt learned its lesson the hard way. The company's experience also provides an important case study for organizations interested in the effects of hiring overconfident, narcissistic, or psychopathic leaders instead of calm, diplomatic, and empathetic ones. With the world's greater awareness of the problems of toxic leadership, people like Khosrowshahi will be more likely to become the preferred leaders—even when they are men.

Ultimately, organizations must decide: if they want to promote a social justice agenda, then the focus on gender representation as an end goal is warranted. But if their goal is to be more effective and successful as an organization, then they should take a comprehensive and critical look at all the leaders they are promoting, not just the women.

Doing so will create the collateral benefit of boosting the proportion of women in leadership. Incidentally, this path will also increase the representation of competent men in leadership roles, as men too are currently disadvantaged by the same toxic criteria that stop talented women from becoming leaders.

When perceptions trump reality

Although this book has devoted substantial attention to the scientific evidence in support of a more gender-balanced leadership representation, the biases and stereotypes that underpin the culture and norms of organizations are no doubt largely immune to such evidence. To put it bluntly, even the most compelling scientific evidence will be eclipsed by the power of perceptions, particularly when perceptions have the power to create an alternative reality.

For instance, Frank Dobbin and Jiwook Jung from Harvard University analyzed a longitudinal data set on the gender composition of boards and on company performance for four hundred large US firms.[9] Their results showed that although adding more women to boards did not change the firms' performance, it led to a *decrease* in the firms' stock valuation. These findings highlight an alarming reality: irrespective of the actual performance differences between men and women, people—and, in this case, investors—are unlikely to change their beliefs, and beliefs drive decisions.

As a result, women are trapped in a vicious cycle whereby their advancement is interpreted as counterproductive to the organization. This impression in turn either hinders their advancement or makes their advancement counterproductive. It is already hard to change perceptions, but when reality is controlled by perceptions, the challenge is monumental. In the infamous words of a senior adviser to George W. Bush, "We're an empire now, and when we act, we create our own reality. And while you're studying that reality—judiciously, as you will—we'll act again, creating other new realities, which you can study too, and that's how things will sort out."[10]

The adviser's admission is shocking only because of how honest it is. Usually, those who control the rules of the game are a bit less transparent about their influence, and the obfuscation increases people's belief in the fairness of the system. Sadly, the winners not only rewrite history, but also create reality, and with that power comes the ability to resist any paradigmatic changes, no matter how rational and fact-based they are.

Primarily for this reason, the economic benefits of greater gender diversity have been hard to demonstrate. To be sure, and to the chagrin of passionate diversity advocates, the assumption that "mixing it up" is advantageous per se has not been backed up with much rigorous data. Much of the evidence of positive links between diversity and financial performance (e.g., returns on equity, revenues, and profits) simply compares highly successful companies with their less successful competitors. Since the successful firms are generally more diverse than the unsuccessful ones, observers assume that diversity drives this success gap. However, this type of evidence ignores the potential effects of other variables (e.g., company culture, leadership quality, and employee engagement) or the possibility of an inverted causal direction—that is, successful companies are more likely to care about diversity, perhaps because they are successful enough to afford dealing with this issue.[11]

Scientific meta-analyses published in independent peer-reviewed journals, rather than companies' white papers, overcome these limitations and provide a much better estimate of the effects of gender diversity on team and firm performance. The results suggest great variability between firms and industries, with diversity having positive but very small effects on performance overall—so small that the overall correlation between diversity and performance is almost zero. In some reviewed studies, diversity even had a negative effect on performance. For instance, Renee Adams from the University of Queensland and Daniel Ferreira from the London School of Economics examined the link between diversity and firm performance in around two thousand US firms. Although they initially found that firms with a higher proportion of female directors tended to show stronger financial results, a more granular analysis revealed that this effect was simply a function of the better monitoring committees that high-performing firms had in place. In fact, among high-performing teams with such committees, a higher proportion of female directors actually decreased firm performance.[12] Why? Investors—who are really just a proxy for the market—consider the presence of more female directors a liability.

It's the talent, stupid

Progress is no straight line, and there's still much progress to be made when it comes to gender diversity, particularly at the top of organizations, where people's performance matters the most because it determines the success of everyone else. The good news is that we are in a better place today than we were fifty years ago. Most notably, the proportion of women at work is much higher today and still growing; women have closed the health and education gap in most countries and even surpassed men in education throughout much of the developed world. Many in-demand college degrees, such as business, law, and medicine, are far less gender segregated than they were, and in most parts of the world, overt dis-crimination is not just less common, but also illegal.[13]

The bad news is that there is still much progress to be made. As the *Economist* noted recently, as many as 104 countries still have labor laws that explicitly ban women from certain jobs.[14] The World Economic Forum estimates that at the current rate of salary growth, we will have to wait another 217 years to achieve global salary parity between men and women.[15] That's not until the year 2235.

If we want better and more effective organizations and societies, we first and foremost need to improve the quality of our leaders. Compelling evidence suggests that leadership is more likely to improve if we start drawing more heavily from the female talent pool, especially if we understand that the women most likely to drive positive change look quite different from the typical leaders we have today, irrespective of gender. But even more critically, we must put in place much bigger obstacles for the disproportionate glut of incompetent men who are so adept at becoming leaders, to everyone's peril.

Notes

Chapter 1

1. Jennifer Robinson, "Turning Around Employee Turnover," *Gallup Business Journal*, May 8, 2008, http://news.gallup.com/businessjournal/106912/turning-around-your-turnover-problem.aspx.

2. Christopher Zara, "People Were Asked to Name Women Tech Leaders. They Said 'Alexa' and 'Siri,'" *Fast Company*, March 20, 2018, www.fastcompany.com/40547212/people-were-asked-to-name-women-tech-leaders-they-said-alexa-and-siri.

3. Judith Warner and Danielle Corley, "The Women's Leadership Gap," *Center for American Progress*, May 21, 2017, www.americanprogress.org/issues/women/reports/2017/05/21/432758/womens-leadership-gap.

4. Tomas Chamorro-Premuzic, "Why Do So Many Incompetent Men Become Leaders?," *Harvard Business Review*, August 22, 2013, https://hbr.org/2013/08/why-do-so-many-incompetent-men.

5. Alice H. Eagly, "When Passionate Advocates Meet Research on Diversity, Does the Honest Broker Stand a Chance?," *Journal of the Society for the Psychological Study of Social Issues* 72, no. 1 (2016): 199–222, https://doi.org/10.1111/josi.12163.

6. Jazmine Boatman and Richard S. Wellins, *Global Leadership Forecast* (Pittsburgh, PA: Development Dimensions International, 2011).

7. Boris Groysberg and Deborah Bell, "Talent Management: Boards Give Their Companies an 'F,'" *Harvard Business Review*, May 28, 2013, https://hbr.org/2013/05/talent-management-boards-give.

8. The Data Team, "What the World Worries About," *Economist*, November 24, 2016, www.economist.com/blogs/graphicdetail/2016/11/daily-chart-17.

9. Manfred F. R. Kets de Vries, "Do You Hate Your Boss?," *Harvard Business Review*, December 2016, https://hbr.org/2016/12/do-you-hate-your-boss.

10. Catherine Clifford, "Unhappy Workers Cost the U.S. Up to $5 Billion a Year," *Entrepreneur*, May 10, 2015, https://www.entrepreneur.com/article/246036.

11. Alice H. Eagly, Mary C. Johannesen-Schmidt, and Marloes L. van Engen, "Transformational, Transactional, and Laissez-Faire Leadership Styles: A Meta-Analysis Comparing Women and Men," *Psychological Bulletin* 129, no. 4 (2003): 569–591.

12. Ibid.

13. Alexander W. Watts, "Why Does John Get the STEM Job Rather than Jennifer?" *Stanford University*, June 2, 2014, https://gender.stanford.edu/news-publications/gender-news/why-does-john-get-stem-job-rather-jennifer.

14. Evelyn Orr and Jane Stevenson, "What Makes Women CEOs Different?" Korn Ferry Institute, November 8, 2017, https://www.kornferry.com/institute/women-ceo-insights.

15. Ohio State University, "Narcissistic People Most Likely to Emerge As Leaders," Newswise, October 7, 2008, www.newswise.com//articles/view/545089.

16. Eugene Webb, *The Self Between: From Freud to the New Social Psychology of France* (London: University of Washington Press, 1993).

Chapter 2

1. Francis Dao, "Without Confidence, There Is No Leadership," *Inc.*, March 1, 2008, www.inc.com/resources/leadership/articles/20080301/dao.html.

2. Victor Lipman, "Why Confidence Is Always a Leader's Best Friend," *Forbes*, May 9, 2017, www.forbes.com/sites/victorlipman/2017/05/09/why-confidence-is-always-a-leaders-best-friend/#27892c9047be.

3. Peter O'Conner, "Introverts Make Great Leaders—But Lack Confidence in Their Capabilities," *Quartz*, October 7, 2017, https://qz.com/1097276/introverts-make-great-leaders-but-lack-confidence-in-their-capabilities.

4. Joseph Pearlman, "How to Exude Confidence Even If You Don't Feel It," *Inc.*, June 28, 2016, www.inc.com/joseph-pearlman/this-simple-mindset-tweak-is-behind-richard-bransons-success.html.

5. Matt Mayberry, "The Incredible Power of Believing in Yourself," *Entrepreneur*, May 29, 2015, www.entrepreneur.com/article/246720.

6. Philipp Alexander Freund and Nadine Kasten, "How Smart Do You Think You Are? A Meta-Analysis on the Validity of Self-Estimates of Cognitive Ability," *Psychological Bulletin* 138, no. 2 (2012): 296–321, https://doi.org/10.1037/a0026556.

7. Luis Santos-Pinto, "Labor Market Signaling and Self-Confidence: Wage Compression and the Gender Pay Gap," *Journal of Labor Economics* 30, no. 4 (2012): 873–914, https://doi.org/10.1086/666646.

8. Heike Heidemeier and Klaus Moser, "Self-Other Agreement in Job Performance Ratings: A Meta-Analytic Test of a Process Model," *Journal of Applied Psychology* 94, no. 2 (2009): 353–370, https://doi.org/10.1037/0021-9010.94.2.353.

9. Gus Lubin, "A Simple Logic Question That Most Harvard Students Get Wrong," *Business Insider*, December 11, 2012, www.businessinsider.com/question-that-harvard-students-get-wrong-2012-12?international=true&r=US&IR=T.

10. Justin Kruger and David Dunning, "Unskilled and Unaware of It: How Difficulties in Recognizing One's Own Incompetence Lead to Inflated Self-Assessments," *Journal of Personality and Social Psychology* 77, no. 6 (1999): 1121–1134.

11. David Dunning et al., "Why People Fail to Recognize Their Own Incompetence," *Current Directions in Psychological Science* 12, no. 3 (2003): 83–87.

12. Bertrand Russell, "The Triumph of Stupidity," in *Mortals and Others: Bertrand Russell's American Essays, 1931–1935*, ed. Harry Ruja (London: Allen and Unwin, 1975–1998), 2:28, available at http://russell-j.com/0583TS.HTM.

13. Heidemeier and Moser, "Self-Other Agreement."

14. S. J. Heine et al., "Is There a Universal Need for Positive Self-Regard?," *Psychological Review* 106, no. 4 (1999): 766–794, https://doi.org/10.1037/0033-295X.106.4.766.

15. Robert Trivers, "The Elements of a Scientific Theory of Self-Deception," *Annals of the New York Academy of Sciences* 907, no. 1(2000): 114–131, https://doi.org/10.1111/j.1749-6632.2000.tb06619.x.

16. Kenny Phua, T. Mandy Tham, and Chi Shen Wei, "Are Overconfident CEOs Better Leaders? Evidence from Stakeholder Commitments," *Journal of Financial Economics* 127, no. 3 (2017): 519–545, https://doi.org/10.1016/j.jfineco.2017.12.008.

17. C. Randall Colvin and Jack Block, "Do Positive Illusions Foster Mental Health? An Examination of the Taylor and Brown Formulation," *Psychological Bulletin* 116, no. 1 (1994): 3–20, https://doi.org/10.1037/0033-2909.116.1.3.

18. Erin Stepp, "More Americans Willing to Ride in Fully Self-Driving Cars," *NewsRoom*, January 24, 2018, http://newsroom.aaa.com/2018/01/americans-willing-ride-fully-self-driving-cars.

19. Nathan Bomey, "U.S. Vehicle Deaths Topped 40,000 in 2017, National Safety Council Estimates," *USA Today*, February 15, 2018, www.usatoday.com/story/money/cars/2018/02/15/national-safety-council-traffic-deaths/340012002.

20. Catherine H. Tinsley and Robin J. Ely, "What Most People Get Wrong About Men and Women," *Harvard Business* Review, May–June, 2018, https://hbr.org/2018/05/what-most-people-get-wrong-about-men-and-women.

21. Laura Guillén, Margarita Mayo, and Natalina Karelaia, "Appearing Self-Confident and Getting Credit for It: Why It May Be Easier for Men than Women to Gain Influence at Work," *Human Resource Management* 57, no. 4 (2017): 839–854, https://doi.org/10.1002/hrm.21857.

22. Karen S. Lyness and Angela R. Grotto, "Women and Leadership in the United States: Are We Closing the Gender Gap?," *Annual Review of Organizational Psychology and Organizational Behavior* 5 (2018): 227–265, https://doi.org/10.1146/annurev-orgpsych.

23. Tinsley, "What Most People Get Wrong."

24. Stepp, "More Americans Willing to Ride."

25. Ernesto Reuben et al., "The Emergence of Male Leadership in Competitive Environments," *Journal of Economic Behavior & Organization* 83, no. 1 (2012): 111–117, https://doi.org/10.1016/j.jebo.2011.06.016.

26. Luís Santos-Pinto, "Labor Market Signaling and Self-Confidence: Wage Compression and the Gender Pay Gap," *Journal of Labor Economics* 30, no. 4 (2012): 873–914, https://doi.org/10.1086/666646.

27. Rachel Feintzeig, "Everything Is Awesome! Why You Can't Tell Employees They're Doing a Bad Job," *Wall Street Journal*, February 10, 2015, www.wsj.com/articles/everything-is-awesome-why-you-cant-tell-employees-theyre-doing-a-bad-job-1423613936.

28. Cheri Ostroff, Leanne E. Atwater, and Barbara J. Feinberg, "Understanding Self-Other Agreement: A Look at Rater and Ratee Characteristics, Context, and Outcomes," *Personnel Psychology* 57, no. 2 (2004): 333–375, https://doi.org/10.1111/j.1744-6570.2004.tb02494.x.

Chapter 3

1. Walter Isaacson, *Steve Jobs* (New York: Simon & Schuster, 2004), 112.

2. Patrick M. Wright et al., "CEO Narcissism, CEO Humility, and C-Suite Dynamics," Center for Executive Succession, 2016, https://pdfs.semanticscholar.org/2abd/a21c7fe916e9030fccbb0b43b45da5da2dec.pdf.

3. Although there is a thin line between narcissism as a clinical, medical diagnosis and narcissism as a layperson's description of egocentric tendencies, this chapter will focus only on the nonclinical definition. Any reference to narcissism or narcissistic individuals or leaders should be understood as relatively functional and nonpathological and therefore free of any suggestions that the person in question requires psychological treatment or must be institutionalized (even if that is still the case).

4. Sara Konrath, Broam P. Meier, and Brad J. Bushman, "Development and Validation of the Single Item Narcissism Scale (SINS)," *PLoS One* 9, no. 8 (2014), https://doi.org/10.1371/journal.pone.0103469.

5. Arijit Chatterjee and Donald C. Hambrick, "It's All About Me: Narcissistic CEOs and Their Effects on Company Strategy and Performance," *Administrative Science Quarterly* 52, no. 3 (2007), 351–386.

6. Charles A. O'Reilly et al., "Narcissistic CEOs and Executive Compensation," *Leadership Quarterly* 25 (2014): 218–231.

7. Laura E. Buffardi and W. Keith Campbell, "Narcissism and Social Networking Web Sites," *Personality and Social Psychology Bulletin* 34, no. 10 (2008): 1303–1314.

8. Ashley L. Watts et al., "The Double-Edged Sword of Grandiose Narcissism: Implications for Successful and Unsuccessful Leadership Among U.S. Presidents," *Psychological Science* 24, no. 12 (2013): 2379–2389, https://doi.org/10.1177/0956797613491970.

9. Amy B. Brunell et al., "Leader Emergence: The Case of the Narcissistic Leader," *Personality and Social Psychology Bulletin* 34, no. 12 (2008): 1663–1676, https://doi.org/10.1177/0146167208324101.

10. Klaus J. Templer, "Why Do Toxic People Get Promoted? For the Same Reason Humble People Do: Political Skill," *Harvard Business Review*, July 10, 2018, https://hbr.org/2018/07/why-do-toxic-people-get-promoted-for-the-same-reason-humble-people-do-political-skill.

11. Emily Grijalva et al., "Narcissism and Leadership: A Meta-Analytic Review of Linear and Nonlinear Relationships," *Personnel Psychology* 68, no. 1 (2015): 1–47, https://doi.org/10.1111/peps.12072.

12. Emily Grijalva et al., "Gender Differences in Narcissism: A Meta-Analytic Review," *Psychological Bulletin* 141, no. 2 (2015): 261–310, https://doi.org/10.1037/a0038231.

13. Ibid.

14. Ibid.

15. Timothy A. Judge, Beth A. Livingston, and Charlice Hurst, "Do Nice Guys—and Gals—Really Finish Last? The Joint Effects of Sex and Agreeableness on Income," *Journal of Personality and Social Psychology* 102, no. 2 (2012): 390–407, https://doi.org/10.1037/a0026021.

16. Barbara Nevicka et al., "Narcissistic Leaders: An Asset or a Liability? Leader Visibility, Follower Responses, and Group-Level Absenteeism," *Journal of Applied Psychology* 103, no. 7 (2018): 703–723; https://doi.org/10.1037/apl0000298.

17. Virgil Zeigler-Hill et al., "The Dark Triad and Sexual Harassment Proclivity," *Personality and Individual Differences* 89 (2016): 47–54, https://doi.org/10.1016/j.paid.2015.09.048.

18. Nihat Aktas et al., "CEO Narcissism and the Takeover Process: From Private Initiation to Deal Completion," *Journal of Financial and Quantitative Analysis* 51, no. 1 (2016): 113–137, https://doi.org/10.1017/S0022109016000065.

19. Frederick L. Coolidge, Linda L. Thede, and Kerry L Jang, "Heritability of Personality Disorders in Children: A Preliminary Investigation," *Journal of Personality Disorders* 15, no. 1 (2001): 33–40, https://doi.org/10.1521/pedi.15.1.33.18645.

20. Robert D. Hare, "The Predators Among Us," keynote address, Canadian Police Association Annual General Meeting, St. John's, Newfoundland and Labrador, August 27, 2002.

21. Paul Babiak, Craig S. Neumann, and Robert D. Hare, "Corporate Psychopathy: Talking the Walk," *Behavioral Sciences and the Law* 28, no. 2 (2010): 174–193, https://doi.org/10.1002/bsl.925.

22. Australian Psychological Society, "Corporate Psychopaths Common and Can Wreak Havoc in Business, Researcher Says," press release, September 13, 2016, www.psychology.org.au/news/media_releases/13September2016/Brooks.

23. Farah Ali and Tomas Chamorro-Premuzic, "The Dark Side of Love and Life Satisfaction: Associations with Intimate Relationships, Psychopathy and Machiavellianism," *Personality and Individual Differences* 48, no. 2 (2010):228–233, https://doi.org/10.1016/j.paid.2009.10.016.

24. Farah Ali and Tomas Chamorro-Premuzic, "Investigating Theory of Mind Deficits in Nonclinical Psychopathy and Machiavellianism," *Personality and Individual Differences* 49, no. 3 (2010), https://doi.org/10.1016/j.paid.2010.03.027.

25. Sarah Francis Smith and Scott O. Lilienfeld, "Psychopathy in the Workplace: The Knowns and Unknowns," *Aggression and Violent Behavior* 18, no. 2 (2013): 204–218, https://doi.org/10.1016/j.avb.2012.11.007.

26. NBC News, "Tsunami Hero Arrested in Australia," *NBCNews.com*, January 3, 2005, www.nbcnews.com/id/6783310/ns/world_news-tsunami_a_year_later/t/tsunami-hero-arrested-australia/#.W4GNVehKhPY.

27. Sarah Francis Smith et al., "Are Psychopaths and Heroes Twigs Off the Same Branch? Evidence from College, Community, and Presidential Samples," *Journal of Research in Personality* 47, no. 5 (2013): 634–646, https://doi.org/10.1016/j.jrp.2013.05.006.

28. J. E. Rogstad and R. Rogers, "Clinical Psychology Review Gender Differences in Contributions of Emotion to Psychopathy and Antisocial Personality Disorder," *Clinical Psychology Review* 28, no. 8 (2008): 1472–1484, https://doi.org/10.1016/j.cpr.2008.09.004.

29. Serena Borroni et al., "Psychopathy Dimensions, Big Five Traits, and Dispositional Aggression in Adolescence: Issues of Gender Consistency," *Personality and Individual Differences* 66 (2014): 199–203, https://doi.org/10.1016/j.paid.2014.03.019.

30. Ellison M. Cale and Scott O. Lilienfeld, "Sex Differences in Psychopathy and Antisocial Personality Disorder: A Review and Integration," *Clinical Psychology Review* 22 (2002): 1179–1207, https://doi.org/10.1016/S0272-7358(01)00125-8.

31. Aliya Ram and Cynthia O'Murchu, "Cambridge Analytica Chief Accused of Taking $8M Before Collapse," *Financial Times*, June 5, 2018, www.ft.com/content/1c8a5e74-6901-11e8-8cf3-0c230fa67aec.

32. Cynthia Mathieu et al., "Corporate Psychopathy and the Full-Range Leadership Model," *Assessment* 22, no. 3 (2015): 267–278, https://doi.org/10.1177/1073191114545490.

33. Ernest H. O'Boyle et al., "A Meta-Analysis of the Dark Triad and Work Behavior: A Social Exchange Perspective," *Journal of Applied Psychology* 97, no. 3 (2012): 557–579, https://doi.org/10.1037/a0025679.

34. Paul Babiak, Craig S. Neumann, and Robert D. Hare, "Corporate Psychology: Talking the Walk," *Behavioral Sciences and the Law* 28 (2010): 174–193, https://doi.org/10.1002/bsl.925.

35. Cynthia Mathieu et al., "A Dark Side of Leadership: Corporate Psychopathy and Its Influence on Employee Well-Being and Job Satisfaction," *Personality and Individual Differences* 59 (2014): 83–88, https://doi.org/10.1016/j.paid.2013.11.010.

36. O'Boyle et al., "Dark Triad and Work Behavior."

37. Michael Housman and Dylan Minor, "Toxic Workers," working paper 16-047, Harvard Business School, Boston, 2015, 1–29.

38. Diana B. Henriques, "Examining Bernie Madoff, 'The Wizard of Lies,'" *Fresh Air*, NPR, April 26, 2011, www.npr.org/2011/04/26/135706926/examining-bernie-madoff-the-wizard-of-lies.

39. Adrian Furnham, Yasmine Daoud, and Viren Swami, "'How to Spot a Psychopath': Lay Theories of Psychopathy," *Social Psychiatry and Psychiatric Epidemiology* 44, no. 6 (2009): 464–472, https://doi.org/10.1007/s00127-008-0459-1.

40. O'Boyle et al., "Dark Triad and Work Behavior."

41. Cynthia Mathieu and Paul Babiak, "What Are the Effects of Psychopathic Traits in a Supervisor on Employees' Psychological Distress?," *Journal of Organizational Culture, Communications and Conflict* 16, no. 2 (2012): 81–85.

42. Daniel N. Jones and Delroy L. Paulhus, "Introducing the Short Dark Triad (SD3): A Brief Measure of Dark Personality Traits," *Assessment* 21, no. 1 (2013): 28–41, https://doi.org/10.1177/1073191113514105.

43. Jesse Fox and Margaret C. Rooney, "The Dark Triad and Trait Self-Objectification As Predictors of Men's Use and Self-Presentation Behaviors on Social Networking Sites," *Personality and Individual Differences* 76 (2015): 161–165, https://doi.org/10.1016/j.paid.2014.12.017.

44. Johann Endres, "The Language of the Psychopath: Characteristics of Prisoners' Performance in a Sentence Completion Test," *Criminal Behavior and Mental Health* 14, no. 3 (2004): 214–226, https://doi.org/10.1002/cbm.588.

45. Bill Steele, "The Words of Psychopaths Reveal Their Predatory Nature," *Cornell Chronicle*, October 17, 2011, http://news.cornell.edu/stories/2011/10/words-psychopaths-reveal-their-predatory-nature.

Chapter 4

1. Adapted from Linda L. Carli and Alice H. Eagly, "Leadership and Gender," in *The Nature of Leadership*, ed. John Antonakis and David V. Day, 2nd ed. (Thousand Oaks, CA: SAGE, 2012), 437–476.

2. "Behind the Mask of Zara: The Management Style of Amancio Ortega," *Economist*, December 17, 2016, www.economist.com/news/business/21711948-founder-inditex-has-become-worlds-second-richest-man-management-style-amancio.

3. "Self-Made Man. Obituary: Ingvar Kamprad Died on January 27th," *Economist*, February 8, 2018, www.economist.com/news/obituary/21736501-founder-ikea-furniture-empire-was-91-obituary-ingvar-kamprad-died-january-27th.

4. Jena McGregor, "The Rundown on Mary Barra, First Female CEO of General Motors," *Washington Post*, December 10, 2013, www.washingtonpost.com/news/on-leadership/wp/2013/12/10/the-rundown-on-mary-barra-first-female-ceo-of-general-motors/?utm_term=.bf017ee125e3.

5. Joann Muller, "Marry Barra Is Running GM with a Tight Fist and an Urgent Mission," *Forbes*, May 2, 2017, www.forbes.com/sites/joannmuller/2017/05/02/mary-barra-is-running-gm-with-a-tight-fist-and-an-urgent-mission/#784fc0691bdb.

6. Bradley P. Owens and David R. Hekman, "How Does Leader Humility Influence Team Performance? Exploring the Mechanisms of Contagion and Collective Promotion Focus," *Academy of Management Journal* 59, no. 3 (2015): 1088–1111, https://doi.org/10.5465/amj.2013.0660.

7. Margarita Mayo, "If Humble People Make the Best Leaders, Why Do We Fall for Charismatic Narcissists?," *Harvard Business Review*, April 7, 2017, https://hbr.org/2017/04/if-humble-people-make-the-best-leaders-why-do-we-fall-for-charismatic-narcissists?utm_campaign=hbr&utm_source=facebook&utm_medium=social.

8. Mansour Javidan et al., "In the Eye of the Beholder: Cross Cultural Lessons in Leadership from Project GLOBAL," *Academy of Management Perspectives* 20, no. 1 (2006): 6790, https://doi.org/10.5465/AMP.2006.19873410.

9. Konstantin O. Tskhay, Rebecca Zhu, and Nicholas O. Rule, "Perceptions of Charisma from Thin Slices of Behavior Predict Leadership Prototypicality Judgments," *Leadership Quarterly* 28, no. 4 (2017): 555–562, https://doi.org/10.1016/j.leaqua.2017.03.003.

10. James W. Beck, Alison E. Carr, and Philip T. Walmsley, "What Have You Done for Me Lately? Charisma Attenuates the Decline in U.S. Presidential Approval over Time," *Leadership Quarterly* 23, no. 5 (2012): 934–942, https://doi.org/10.1016/j.leaqua.2012.06.002.

11. Robert Hogan, Gordon J. Curphy, and Joyce Hogan, "What We Know About Leadership," *American Psychologist* (1994): 493–504, https://pdfs.semanticscholar.org/a705/2f29f15cb4c8c637f0dc0b505793b37575d7.pdf.

12. Jay A. Conger, "The Dark Side of Leadership," *Organizational Dynamics* 19, no. 2 (1990): 44–55, https://doi.org/10.1016/0090-2616(90)90070-6.

13. Prasad Balkundi, Martin Kilduff, and David A. Harrison, "Centrality and Charisma: Comparing How Leader Networks and Attributions Affect Team Performance," *Journal of Applied Psychology* 96, no. 6 (2011):1209–1222, https://doi.org/10.1037/a0024890.

14. Robert B. Kaiser and Wanda T. Wallace, "Gender Bias and Substantive Differences in Ratings of Leadership Behavior: Toward a New Narrative," *Consulting Psychology Journal: Practice and Research* 68, no. 1 (2016): 72–98, https://doi.org/10.1037/cpb0000059.

15. Kevin S. Groves, "Gender Differences in Social and Emotional Skills and Charismatic Leadership," *Journal of Leadership and Organizational Studies* 11, no. 3 (2005): 30–46, https://doi.org/10.1177/107179190501100303.

16. Herminia Ibarra and Otilia Obodaru, "Women and the Vision Thing," *Harvard Business Review,* January 2009, https://hbr.org/2009/01/women-and-the-vision-thing.

17. Ronald J. Deluga, "Relationship Among American Presidential Charismatic Leadership, Narcissism, and Rated Performance," *Leadership Quarterly* 8, no. 1 (1997): 49–65, https://doi.org/10.1016/S1048-9843(97)90030-8.

18. Allen Grabo, Brian R. Spisak, Mark van Vugt, "Charisma As Signal: An Evolutionary Perspective on Charismatic Leadership," *Leadership Quarterly* 28, no.4 (2017): 482, https://doi.org/10.1016/j.leaqua.2017.05.001.

19. Beck, Carr, and Walmsley, "What Have You Done for Me Lately?"

20. Henry L. Tosi et al., "CEO Charisma, Compensation, and Firm Performance," *Leadership Quarterly* 15, no. 3 (2004): 405–420.

Chapter 5

1. ExpovistaTV, *Davos 2018: Jack Ma's Keys to Success: Technology, Women, Peace and Never Complain*, videorecording, published January 24, 2018, www.youtube.com/watch?v=-nSbkywGf-E.

2. Janet S. Hyde, "Gender Similarities and Differences," *Annual Review of Psychology* 65, no. 3 (2014): 1–26, https://doi.org/10.1146/annurev-psych-010213-115057.

3. Janet S. Hyde, "The Gender Similarities Hypothesis," *American Psychologist* 60, no. 6 (2005): 581–592, https://doi.org/10.1037/0003-066X.60.6.581.

4. David I. Miller and Diane F. Halpern, "The New Science of Cognitive Sex Differences," *Trends in Cognitive Sciences* 18, no. 1 (2014): 37–45, https://doi.org/10.1016/j.tics.2013.10.011.

5. Alice H. Eagly, Mary C. Johannesen-Schmidt, and Marloes L. van Engen, "Transformational, Transactional, and Laissez-Faire Leadership Styles: A Meta-Analysis Comparing Women and Men," *Psychological Bulletin* 129, no. 4 (2003): 569–591.

6. Rong Su, James Rounds, and Patrick I. Armstrong, "Men and Things, Women and People: A Meta-Analysis of Sex Differences in Interests," *Psychological Bulletin* 135, no. 6 (2009): 859–884, https://doi.org/10.1037/a0017364.

7. James Danmore, "Google's Ideological Echo Chamber: How Bias Clouds Our Thinking About Diversity and Inclusion," internal memo to Google personnel, July 2017, cited in Louise Matsakis, Jason Koebler, and Sarah Emerson, "Here Are the Citations for the Anti-Diversity Manifesto Circulating at Google," *Motherboard*, updated August 7, 2017, https://motherboard.vice.com/en_us/article/evzjww/here-are-the-citations-for-the-anti-diversity-manifesto-circulating-at-google.

8. Robert Hogan, Tomas Chamorro-Premuzic, and Robert B. Kaiser, "Employability and Career Success: Bridging the Gap Between Theory and Reality," *Industrial and Organizational Psychology* 6, no. 1 (2013): 3–16, https://doi.org/10.1111/iops.12001.

9. Reece Akhtar et al., "The Engageable Personality: Personality and Trait EI As Predictors of Work Engagement," *Personality and Individual Differences* 73 (2015): 44–49, https://doi.org/10.1016/j.paid.2014.08.040.

10. Simon Baron-Cohen et al., "The Autism-Spectrum Quotient (AQ): Evidence from Asperger Syndrome/High-Functioning Autism, Males and Females, Scientists and Mathematicians," *Journal of Autism and Developmental Disorders* 31, no. 1 (2001): 5–17, https://doi.org/10.1023/A:1005653411471.

11. Dana L. Joseph and Daniel A. Newman, "Emotional Intelligence: An Integrative Meta-Analysis and Cascading Model," *Journal of Applied Psychology* 95, no. 1 (2010): 54–78, https://doi.org/10.1037/a0017286.

12. YoungHee Hur, Peter T. van den Berg, and Celeste P. M. Wilderom, "Transformational Leadership As a Mediator Between Emotional Intelligence and Team Outcomes," *Leadership Quarterly* 22, no. 4 (2011): 591–603, https://doi.org/10.1016/j.leaqua.2011.05.002.

13. Ibid.

14. Jill E. Rogstad and Richard Rogers, "Clinical Psychology Review Gender Differences in Contributions of Emotion to Psychopathy and Antisocial Personality Disorder," *Clinical Psychology Review* 28, no. 8 (2008): 1472–1484, https://doi.org/10.1016/j. cpr.2008.09.004.

15. Sheryl Sandberg and Adam Grant, *Option B: Facing Adversity, Building Resilience, and Finding Joy* (New York: Alfred A. Knopf, 2017).

16. Sarah Green Carmichael, "Sheryl Sandberg and Adam Grant on Resilience," *Harvard Business Review*, April 27, 2017, https://hbr. org/ideacast/2017/04/sheryl-sandberg-and-adam-grant-on-resilience.

17. Velmer S. Burton Jr., et al., "Gender, Self-Control, and Crime," *Journal of Research in Crime and Delinquency* 35, no. 2 (1998): 123–147, doi:10.1177/0022427898035002001.

18. Sylvia Ann Hewlett, "Women on Boards: America Is Falling Behind," *Harvard Business Review*, May 3, 2011, https://hbr. org/2011/05/women-on-boards-america.

19. Sari M. van Anders, Jeffrey Steiger, and Katherine L. Goldey, "Effects of Gendered Behavior on Testosterone in Women and Men," *Proceedings of the National Academy of Sciences of the United States of America* 112, no. 45 (2015): 13805–13810, https://doi.org/10.1073/ pnas.1509591112.

20. Clive Fletcher, "The Implications of Research on Gender Differences in Self-Assessment and 360 Degree Appraisal," *Human Resource Management Journal* 9, no. 1 (1999): 39–46, https://doi. org/10.1111/j.1748-8583.1999.tb00187.x.

Chapter 6

1. See https://en.wikipedia.org/wiki/List_of_best-selling_books.

2. Amanda H. Goodall, Lawrence M. Kahn, and Andrew J. Oswald, "Why Do Leaders Matter? A Study of Expert

Knowledge in a Superstar Setting," *Journal of Economic Behavior and Organization* 77, no. 3 (2011): 265–284, https://doi.org/10.1016/j. jebo.2010.11.001; Amanda H. Goodall and Ganna Pogrebna, "Expert Leaders in a Fast-Moving Environment," *Leadership Quarterly* 26, no. 2 (2015): 123–142, https://doi.org/10.1016/j. leaqua.2014.07.009.

3. Amanda H. Goodall, "Highly Cited Leaders and the Performance of Research Universities," *Research Policy* 38, no. 7 (2009): 1079–1092, https://doi.org/10.1016/j.respol.2009.04.00.

4. Benjamin Artz, Amanda H. Goodall, and Andrew J. Oswald, "If Your Boss Could Do Your Job, You're More Likely to Be Happy at Work," *Harvard Business Review*, December 29, 2016, https://hbr. org/2016/12/if-your-boss-could-do-your-job-youre-more-likely-to-be-happy-at-work.

5. Thomas W. H. Ng and Daniel C. Feldman, "How Broadly Does Education Contribute to Job Performance?," *Personnel Psychology* 62 (2009): 89–134, https://doi.org/10.1111/j.1744-6570.2008.01130.x.

6. Prasad Balkundi and Martin Kilduff, "The Ties That Lead: A Social Network Approach to Leadership," *Leadership Quarterly* 17, no. 4 (2006): 419–439.

7. Dimitrios C. Christopoulos, "The Impact of Social Networks on Leadership Behaviour," *Methodological Innovations* 9 (2016): 1–15, https://doi.org/10.1177/2059799116630649.

8. Frank L. Schmidt, In-Sue Oh, and Jonathan A. Shaffer, "The Validity and Utility of Selection Methods in Personnel Psychology: Practical and Theoretical Implications of 100 Years of Research Findings," working paper, October 2016, https://home.ubalt.edu/ tmitch/645/articles/2016-100%20Yrs%20Working%20Paper%20 for%20Research%20Gate%2010-17.pdf.

9. Matthew Stewart, "The 9.9 Percent Is the New American Aristocracy," *Atlantic*, June 2018, www.theatlantic.com/magazine/ archive/2018/06/the-birth-of-a-new-american-aristocracy/559130.

10. Lauren Leatherby, "US Social Mobility Gap Continues to Widen," *Financial Times*, December 16, 2016, www.ft.com/ content/7de9165e-c3d2-11e6-9bca-2b93a6856354.

11. Tomas Chamorro-Premuzic, *The Talent Delusion: Why Data, Not Intuition, Is the Key to Unlocking Human Potential* (London: Piatkus, 2017).

12. Timothy A. Judge et al., "Personality and Leadership: A Qualitative and Quantitative Review," *Journal of Applied Psychology*

87, no. 4 (2002): 765–780, https://doi.org/10.1037//0021-9010.
87.4.765.

13. Timothy A. Judge, Amy E. Colbert, and Remus Ilies,
"Intelligence and Leadership: A Quantitative Review and Test of
Theoretical Propositions," *Journal of Applied Psychology* 89, no. 3
(2004): 542–552, doi: 10.1037/0021-9010.89.3.542.

14. Full disclosure: I acted as Hogan's CEO in past years and still
maintain a close association with the firm.

15. Robert Hogan and Tomas Chamorro-Premuzic, "Personality
and the Laws of History," in *The Wiley-Blackwell Handbook of
Individual Differences*, ed. Tomas Chamorro-Premuzic, Sophie von
Stumm, and Adrian Furnham (Hoboken, NJ: WileyBlackwell, 2011),
491–511, https://doi.org/10.1002/9781444343120.ch18.

16. Geert Hofstede, Gert Jan Hofstede, and Michael Minkov,
Cultures and Organizations: Software of the Mind, 3rd ed. (New York:
McGraw-Hill, 2010).

17. A great free resource to compare country norms can be found
at Hofstede Insights, "Compare Countries," accessed September 9,
2018, www.hofstede-insights.com/product/compare-countries.

Chapter 7

1. Tomas Chamorro-Premuzic and Gillian Pillans, "Assessing
Potential: From Academic Theories to Practical Realities," *Corporate
Research Forum* (2016): 1–5.

2. Naomi Ellemers, "Gender Stereotypes," *Annual Review of
Psychology* 69 (2018): 275–298.

3. Karen S. Lyness and Angela R. Grotto, "Women and
Leadership in the United States: Are We Closing the Gender Gap?,"
Annual Review or Organizational Psychology and Organizational Behavior
5 (2018): 227–265, https://doi.org/10.1146/annurev-orgpsych-
032117-104739.

4. Julia Levashina et al., "The Structured Employment
Interview: Narrative and Quantitative Review of the Research,"
Personnel Psychology 67, no.1 (2014): 241–293, https://doi.org/10.1111/
peps.12052

5. Frank L. Schmidt and John E. Hunter, "The Validity and
Utility of Selection Methods in Personnel Psychology: Practical
and Theoretical Implications of 85 Years of Research Findings,"

Psychological Bulletin 124, no. 2 (1998): 262–274, https://doi.org/10.1037/0033-2909.124.2.262.

6. Ryan J. Giuliano and Nicole Y. Wicha, "Why the White Bear Is Still There: Electrophysiological Evidence for Ironic Semantic Activation During Thought Suppression," *Brain Research* 1316 (2010): 62–74, https://doi.org/10.1016/j.brainres.2009.12.041.

7. G. L. Stewart et al., "Exploring the Handshake in Employment Interviews," *Journal of Applied Psychology* 93, no. 5 (2008): 1139–1146, https://doi.org/10.1037/0021-9010.93.5.1139.

8. Iris Bohnet, "How to Take the Bias Out of Interviews," *Harvard Business Review*, April 18, 2016, https://hbr.org/2016/04/how-to-take-the-bias-out-of-interviews.

9. Neal Schmitt, "Personality and Cognitive Ability as Predictors of Effective Performance at Work," *Annual Review of Organizational Psychology and Organizational Behavior* 1, no. 1 (2013): 45–65, https://doi.org/10.1146/annurev-orgpsych-031413-091255.

10. Tomas Chamorro-Premuzic and Adran Furhnam, "Intellectual Competence and the Intelligent Personality: A Third Way in Differential Psychology," *Review of General Psychology* 10, no. 3 (2006): 251–267, https://doi.org/10.1037/1089-2680.10.3.251.

11. Benjamin Schneider, Mark G. Ehrhart, and William H. Macey, "Organizational Climate and Culture," *Annual Review of Psychology* 65 (2013): 361–388, https://doi.org/10.1146/annurev-psych-113011-143809.

12. Jasmine Vergauwe et al., "The Too Little/Too Much Scale: A New Rating Format for Detecting Curvilinear Effects," *Organizational Research Methods* 20, no. 3 (2017): 518–544, https://doi.org/10.1177/1094428117706534.

13. Tomas Chamorro-Premuzic et al., "The Datafication of Talent: How Technology Is Advancing the Science of Human Potential at Work," *Current Opinion in Behavioral Sciences* 18 (2017): 13–16, https://doi.org/10.1016/j.cobeha.2017.04.007.

14. Stephen Turban, Laura Freeman, and Ben Waber, "A Study Used Sensors to Show That Men and Women Are Treated Differently at Work," *Harvard Business Review*, October 23, 2017, https://hbr.org/2017/10/a-study-used-sensors-to-show-that-men-and-women-are-treated-differently-at-work.

15. Reece Akhtar and Soong Moon Kang, "The Role of Personality and Social Capital on Intrapreneurial Achievement," *Academy of Management Proceedings* 2016, no. 1 (2017): https://doi.org/10.5465/ambpp.2016.16763abstract.

Chapter 8

1. David V. Day and Lisa Dragoni, "Leadership Development: An Outcome-Oriented Review Based on Time and Levels of Analyses," *Annual Review of Organizational Psychology and Organizational Behavior* 2 (2015): 133–156, https://doi.org/10.1146/annurev-orgpsych-032414-111328.

2. Michael Beer, Magnus Finnström, and Derek Schrader, "Why Leadership Training Fails—and What to Do About It," *Harvard Business Review*, October 2016, https://hbr.org/2016/10/why-leadership-training-fails-and-what-to-do-about-it.

3. Tim Theeboom, Bianca Beersma, and Annelies E. M. van Vianen, "Does Coaching Work? A Meta-Analysis on the Effects of Coaching on Individual Level Outcomes in an Organizational Context," *Journal of Positive Psychology* 9 (2014): 1–18, https://doi.org/10.1080/17439760.2013.837499.

4. Doris B. Collins and Elwood F. Holton III, "The Effectiveness of Managerial Leadership Development Programs: A Meta-Analysis of Studies from 1982 to 2001," *Human Resource Development Quarterly* 15, no. 2 (2004): 217–248, https://doi.org/10.1002/hrdq.1099.

5. Avraham Kluger and Angelo DeNisi, "The Effects of Feedback Interventions on Performance: A Historical Review, a Meta-Analysis, and a Preliminary Feedback Intervention Theory," *Psychological Bulletin* 119, no. 2 (1996): 254–284, https://doi.org/10.1037/0033-2909.119.2.254.

6. Robert B. Kaiser and Cordy Curphy, "Leadership Development: The Failure of an Industry and the Opportunity for Consulting Psychologists," *Consulting Psychology Journal: Practice and Research* 65, no. 4 (2013): 294–302, https://doi.org/10.1037/a0035460.

7. Sorel Cahan and Nora Cohen, "Age Versus Schooling Effects on Intelligence Development," *Child Development* 60, no. 5 (1989): 1239–1249, https://doi.org/10.2307/1130797.

8. Ian J. Deary et al., "Genetic Contributions to Stability and Change in Intelligence from Childhood to Old Age," *Nature* 482 (February 9, 2012): 212–215, https://doi.org/10.1038/nature10781.

9. James M. Olson et al., "The Heritability of Attitudes: A Study of Twins," *Journal of Personality and Social Psychology* 80, no. 6 (2001): 845–846, https://doi.org/10.1037/0022-3514.80.6.845.

10. Richard D. Arvey et al., "The Determinants of Leadership Role Occupancy: Genetic and Personality Factors," *Leadership Quarterly* 17, no. 1 (2006): 1–20, https://doi.org/10.1016/j.leaqua.2005.10.009.

11. Ibid.

12. Brooke N. Macnamara, David Z. Hambrick, and Frederick L. Oswald, "Deliberate Practice and Performance in Music, Games, Sports, Education, and Professions: A Meta-Analysis," *Psychological Science* 25, no. 8 (2014): 1608–1618, https://doi.org/10.1177/0956797614535810.

13. Timothy A. Judge et al., "Personality and Leadership: A Qualitative and Quantitative Review," *Journal of Applied Psychology* 87, no. 4 (2002): 765–780, https://doi.org/10.1037//0021-9010.87.4.765.

14. Ian D. Gow et al, "CEO Personality and Firm Policies," NBER Working Paper Series, no. 22435, July 2016, https://www.hbs.edu/faculty/Pages/item.aspx?num=50477.

15. Douglas T. Hall, Karen L. Otazo, and George P. Hollenbeck, "Behind Closed Doors: What Really Happens in Executive Coaching," *Organ Dynamics* 27, no. 3 (1999): 39–53, https://doi.org/10.1016/S0090-2616(99)90020-7.

16. Erik de Haan, Vicki Culpin, and Judy Curd, "Executive Coaching in Practice: What Determines Helpfulness for Clients of Coaching?," *Personnel Review* 40, no. 1 (2011): 24–4, https://doi.org/10.1108/00483481111095500.

17. Katherine Ely et al., "Evaluating Leadership Coaching: A Review and Integrated Framework," *Leadership Quarterly* 21, no. 4 (2010): 585–599, https://doi.org/10.1016/j.leaqua.2010.06.003.

18. Theeboom, Beersma, and van Vianen, "Does Coaching Work?"

19. Tammi R. A. Kral et al., "Neural Correlates of Video Game Empathy Training in Adolescents: A Randomized Trial," *NPJ Science of Learning* 3, no. 13 (2018), https://doi.org/10.1038/s41539-018-0029-6.

20. Andrew Butler et al., "The Empirical Status of Cognitive-Behavioral Therapy: A Review of Meta-Analyses," *Clinical Psychology Review* 26, no. 1 (2006): 17–31, https://doi.org/10.1016/j.cpr.2005.07.003.

21. Tom Rath, *StrengthsFinder 2.0 from Gallup: Discover Your CliftonStrengths* (New York: Gallup Press, 2016).

22. Kluger and Angelo, "Effects of Feedback Interventions."

23. Allan H. Church et al., "The Role of Personality in Organization Development: A Multi-Level Framework for Applying Personality to Individual, Team, and Organizational Change," in *Research in Organizational Change and Development*, ed. Abraham B. (Rami) Shani and Debra A. Noumair, vol. 23 (Bingley, UK: Emerald Group Publishing, 2015) 91–166, https://doi.org/10.1108/S0897-301620150000023003.

24. Sheila Kampa-Kokesch and Mary Z. Anderson, "Executive Coaching: A Comprehensive Review of the Literature," *Consulting Psychology Journal: Practice and Research* 53, no. 4 (2001): 205–228, https://doi.org/10.1037//1061-4087.53.4.205.

25. James W. Smither et al., "Can Working with an Executive Coach Improve Multisource Feedback Ratings Over Time? A Quasi-Experimental Field Study," *Personnel Psychology* 56 (2003): 23–44, https://doi.org/10.1111/j.1744-6570.2003.tb00142.x.

26. Dan Ariely, *Predictably Irrational: The Hidden Forces That Shape Our Decisions* (New York: Harper, 2008), 294.

27. Janet Polivy and C. Peter Herman, "The False-Hope Syndrome: Unfulfilled Expectations of Self-Change," *Current Directions in Psychological Science* 9, no. 4 (2000): 128–131, https://doi.org/10.1111/1467-8721.00076.

28. Nathan W. Hudson and R. Chris Fraley, "Do People's Desires to Change Their Personality Traits Vary with Age? An Examination of Trait Change Goals Across Adulthood," *Social Psychology and Personality Science* 7, no. 8 (2016): 847–858 https://doi.org/10.1177/1948550616657598.

29. J. A. Dennisen, Marcel A. G. van Aken, and Brent W. Roberts, "Personality Development Across the Life Span," in *The Wiley-Blackwell Handbook of Individual Differences*, ed. Tomas Chamorro-Premuzic, Sophie von Stumm, and Adrian Furnham (Hoboken, NJ: WileyBlackwell, 2011).

30. Zig Ziglar, *See You at the Top, Twenty-Fifth Anniversary Edition*, 2nd rev. ed. (Gretna, LA: Pelican Publishing, 2005), 164.

31. Frederick Anseel et al., "How Are We Doing After 30 Years? A Meta-Analytic Review of the Antecedents and Outcomes of Feedback-Seeking Behavior," *Journal of Management* 41, no. 1 (2015), https://doi.org/10.1177/0149206313484521.

Chapter 9

1. Timothy A. Judge, Ronald F. Piccolo, and Tomek Kosalka, "The Bright and Dark Sides of Leader Traits: A Review and Theoretical Extension of the Leader Trait Paradigm," *Leadership Quarterly* 20, no. 6 (2009): 855–875, https://doi.org/10.1016/j.leaqua.2009.09.004.

2. Timothy A. Judge and Daniel M. Cable, "The Effect of Physical Height on Workplace Success and Income: Preliminary Test of a Theoretical Model," *Journal of Applied Psychology* 89, no. 3 (2004): 428–441, https://doi.org/10.1037/0021-9010.89.3.428.

3. Elaine M. Wong, Margaret E. Ormiston, and Michael P. Haselhuhn, "A Face Only an Investor Could Love: CEOs' Facial Structure Predicts Their Firms' Financial Performance," *Psychological Science* 22, no. 12 (2011): 1478–1483, https://doi.org/10.1177/0956797611418838.

4. Robert Hogan and Tomas Chamorro-Premuzic, "Personality and the Laws of History," in *The Wiley-Blackwell Handbook of Individual Differences*, ed. Tomas Chamorro-Premuzic, Sophie von Stumm, and Adrian Furnham (Hoboken, NJ: WileyBlackwell, 2011), 491–511, https://doi.org/10.1002/9781444343120.ch18.

5. Wendy Wood and Alice H. Eagly, "Biosocial Construction of Sex Differences and Similarities in Behavior," in *Advances in Experimental Social Psychology*, ed. James M. Olson and Mark P. Zanna, vol. 46 (Amsterdam: Elsevier/Academic Press, 2012), https://doi.org/10.1016/B978-0-12-394281-4.00002-7.

6. Emilio J. Castilla and Stephen Bernard, "The Paradox of Meritocracy in Organizations," *Administrative Science Quarterly* 55 (2010): 543–576, available at *DSpace@MIT*, MIT Open Access Articles, December 2012, https://dspace.mit.edu/handle/1721.1/65884.

7. Stephen Benard, "Why His Merit Raise Is Bigger Than Hers," *Harvard Business Review*, April 2012, https://hbr.org/2012/04/why-his-merit-raise-is-bigger-than-hers.

8. Sheelah Kolhatkar, "At Uber, a New C.E.O. Shifts Gears," *New Yorker*, April 9, 2018, www.newyorker.com/magazine/2018/04/09/at-uber-a-new-ceo-shifts-gears.

9. Frank Dobbin and Jiwook Jung, "Corporate Board Gender Diversity and Stock Performance: The Competence Gap or Institutional Investor Bias?," *North Carolina Law Review* 89 (2011): 809–838.

10. Ron Suskind, "Faith, Certainty and the Presidency of George W. Bush," *New York Times Magazine*, October 17, 2004, www.nytimes.com/2004/10/17/magazine/faith-certainty-and-the-presidency-of-george-w-bush.html, attributes the quote to an unnamed "senior adviser to Bush." Mark Danner, "Words in a Time of War: On Rhetoric, Truth and Power," *Mark Danner* (blog), November 2007, www.markdanner.com/articles/words-in-a-time-of-war-on-rhetoric-truth-and-power, says that the quote was by Karl Rove, but Zach Schonfeld, "The Curious Case of a Supposed Karl Rove Quote Used on the National's New Album 'Sleep Well Beast,'" *Newsweek*, September 8, 2017, www.newsweek.com/national-sleep-well-beast-karl-rove-662307, says that Rove denied ever saying these words.

11. Amanda H. Eagly, "When Passionate Advocates Meet Research on Diversity, Does the Honest Broker Stand a Chance?," *Journal of Social Issues* 72, no. 1 (2016): 199–222, https://doi.org/10.1111/josi.12163.

12. Renée B. Adams and Daniel Ferreira, "Women in the Boardroom and Their Impact on Governance and Performance," *Journal of Financial Economics* 94, no. 2 (2009): 291–309, https://doi.org/10.1016/j.jfineco.2008.10.007.

13. Victor E. Sojo et al., "Reporting Requirements, Targets, and Quotas for Women in Leadership," *Leadership Quarterly* 27, no. 3 (2016): 519–536, https://doi.org/10.1016/j.leaqua.2015.12.003.

14. "Labour Laws in 104 Countries Reserve Some Jobs for Men Only," *Economist*, May 26, 2018, www.economist.com/finance-and-economics/2018/05/26/labour-laws-in-104-countries-reserve-some-jobs-for-men-only.

15. "Closing the Gender Gap," *World Economic Forum*, 2018, www.weforum.org/projects/closing-the-gender-gap-gender-parity-task-forces.

Index

Acknowledgments

Thanks to everyone who contributed to this project.

First and foremost, thanks to the amazing Sarah Green Carmichael at *Harvard Business Review* for suggesting the original article that has now grown into this book and for deploying her editorial talents to inject some much-needed order to my otherwise chaotic ruminations. I am very fortunate to have worked with Sarah for several years now; it has been a stimulating and prolific collaboration and I continue to learn a great deal from her.

Second, I would like to thank everyone else at HBR and the Press for always being prompt, professional, and proficient and living up to their stellar reputation. It is a privilege to publish with you.

Third, I would like to thank my agent, Giles Anderson, for making this project happen and for representing my two previous books, *Confidence* and *The Talent Delusion*.

Fourth, I am grateful to Mylene and Isabelle for donating many more hours to the production of this book than I originally requested.

Last, I am grateful to all the incompetent men who become leaders, for they will surely be the number one sales force for this book.

About the Author

TOMAS CHAMORRO-PREMUZIC, PhD, is an international authority on talent management, leadership development, and people analytics. He is the Chief Talent Scientist at ManpowerGroup, cofounder of Metaprofiling and Deeper Signals, and Professor of Business Psychology at both University College London and Columbia University. He has previously held academic positions at New York University and the London School of Economics. He has lectured at Harvard Business School, Stanford Business School, London Business School, Johns Hopkins, and IMD in addition to serving as CEO at Hogan Assessment Systems.

Chamorro-Premuzic has published 10 books and over 150 scientific papers, making him one of the most prolific social scientists of his generation. His work has received awards from the American Psychological Association, the International Society for the Study of Individual Differences, and the Society for Industrial-Organizational Psychology, of which he is a Fellow. He is also the founding director of University College London's

Industrial-Organizational and Business Psychology program and the Chief Psychometric Advisor to Harvard's Entrepreneurial Finance Lab.

Over the past twenty years, Chamorro-Premuzic has consulted for a range of clients in financial services (e.g., J.P. Morgan, HSBC, Goldman Sachs), advertising (e.g., Google, WPP, BBH), media (e.g., BBC, Red Bull, Twitter, Spotify), consumer goods (e.g., Unilever, Reckitt Benckiser, Procter & Gamble), fashion (e.g., LVMH, Net-a-Porter, Valentino), government (e.g., British Army, Royal Mail, NHS), and intergovernmental organizations (e.g., United Nations and World Bank).

Chamorro-Premuzic's media career comprises over 100 TV appearances, including on the BBC, CNN, and Sky, and regular features in *Harvard Business Review*, the *Guardian* (UK edition), *Fast Company*, *Forbes*, and the *Huffington Post*. He is a keynote speaker for the Institute of Economic Affairs. He was born and raised in the Villa Freud district of Buenos Aires but spent most of his professional career in London. He currently lives in Brooklyn, New York. His website is drtomas.com and you can find him on Twitter @drtcp.